Powerful Interactions

HOW TO CONNECT WITH CHILDREN TO EXTEND THEIR LEARNING

Amy Laura Dombro
Judy Jablon, and
Charlotte Stetson

Washington, DC

**Powerful Interactions: How to Connect with Children
to Extend Their Learning**

CREDITS

Book design: J. Michael Myers, www.jmichaelmyersdesign.com.

Photographs: Ken Alswang: *cover, vii, viii, 2, 4, 5, 6, 7, 11, 16, 17, 20, 25, 28, 35, 36, 39, 40, 43, 45, 46, 49, 50, 51, 53, 61, 63, 67, 71, 72, 79, 80, 85, 86, 89, 93, 95, 101, 107, 110, 113, 117, 123, 124, 127, 130, 135, 136, 142, 145.*
Bonnie Blagojevic: *109.* Peg Callaghan: *30.* Judy Jablon: *75, 104, 105, 146.*
Sandra Lighter-Jones: *9, 129.* John Matters: *vi.* Karen Phillips: *37, 65.*
Jude Keith Rose: *91.* Ellen B. Senisi: *57, 114.* Shutterstock.com: *14, 58, 102, 119, 120, 140.* Michael Siluk: *54.* Susan Wagner: *92, 98.*

Library of Congress Control Number: 2011926729
ISBN: 978-1-928896-72-2
NAEYC Item #245

National Association for the Education of Young Children
1313 L Street NW, Suite 500 • Washington, DC 20005-4101
202.232.8777 • 800.424.2460
www.naeyc.org

NAEYC BOOKS STAFF

Editor in Chief, Akimi Gibson
Editorial Director, Bry Pollack
Senior Editor, Holly Bohart
Assistant Editor, Elizabeth Wegner
Editorial Assistant, Ryan Smith
Design and Production, Malini Dominey
Permissions, Lacy Thompson

CONTENTS

ACKNOWLEDGMENTS

We are deeply appreciative to many people who helped us turn our ideas into this book. First and foremost, we acknowledge with great appreciation and respect the children, families, teachers, and colleagues who have taught us so much over the years.

As this book has taken shape over the past two years, we have interacted with some special groups of educators, who allowed us into their classrooms to observe, coach, and take photographs. Through them, we have gained a much deeper understanding of teacher-child interactions. We are extremely grateful to the administrators, teachers, and children in these programs: In New Jersey, the Irvington Preschool program, the East Orange Preschool and Kindergarten program, the Orange Public School kindergartens, the Ben Samuels Children's Center at Montclair State University, and the South Orange YMCA; in New York, the Rockefeller University Children's Center; and in Hawaii, the Kamehameha Preschool Program.

To the teachers who helped to make this book come to life by allowing us to photograph them and their classrooms, a heartfelt thanks: Julia Barney, Johnell Beckles, Annie Julien, Adriana Loffredo, Farah Melbourne, Rose Mary Ortiz, Shelley King Kamara, Brenda Perry and Bernice Mosely, Joie Fields, Aaliyah Graham, Shalkeem Hall, Patricia Fdyfil, Lucy Galante, Lauren Chee, Emily Rodriquez, Wendy Burkins, Robert Milton, Sharon Cohen, Erin Clark, Dana Miuccio, Markeisha Holmes, Auntie Boker, Samantha Edwards, Rory Collin, Sarah Drossman, Karen Zambrano, Jessica Tereskiewicsz, Charles Copeland, Maggie Blezin, Latifah Broadneck-Parker, Lisa McClain, Tijwana Dunkley, Setonya Windham, JoAnn St. Jacques, Kendra King, Teresa Repisack, and Nicki Hines.

Friends and colleagues offered guidance throughout our process. Joan Cenedella read early drafts of our manuscript and helped us clarify the difference between everyday interactions and Powerful Interactions. Laura Herold provided us with research citations, insights about the manuscript, and a photo of her beautiful son Oliver (taken by John Matters), each of which made our book better. When we needed a reviewer, a sounding board, or a rich example from the classroom, Holly Seplocha, Dorothea Marsden, and Louis Romei consistently came through for us; they have our heartfelt thanks.

Our colleagues at NAEYC provided invaluable support to us throughout the development of this book. Akimi Gibson encouraged our vision and guided us to making it a reality; editors Bry Pollack and Holly Bohart forced us to think clearly about our message; and designer Mike Myers transformed our words into the beautiful pages of this book.

We are indebted to our photographer, Ken Alswang, of At Home Studios, for understanding the three steps of Powerful Interactions and helping us to capture our story in photographs. In addition, we extend deep appreciation to Sandra Lighter-Jones, who provided us with beautiful photographs of children and teachers from Kamehameha.

Finally, thanks to our partners, Ed, Andy, and Lesley, for the cream cheese brownies, the concept of "instant replay" that eluded us, and freshly picked garden-by-the-sea produce that inspired and energized us throughout the process of writing this book. Their love and support to each and all three of us made this book possible. ✳

WELCOME

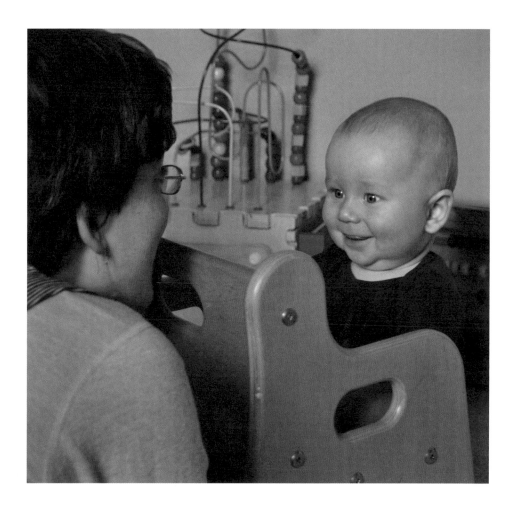

Welcome to a conversation about the power of the interactions you have with children every day.

You may work with young children in a center or your home, in an Early Head Start or Head Start program, in a preschool or an early elementary classroom, or you may be a home visitor. Regardless, this book is for you because you make a difference!

In particular, the decisions you make about how you will interact with children have an impact on them, on their development and learning, today and for the future.

The Power of Teacher-Child Interactions

It was Russian psychologist Lev Vygotsky (1896–1934) who first explained the vital connection between interactions and learning. He explained that as young children act and interact in shared experiences with others, those social interactions play a key role in how children learn to think, reason, and communicate. For this reason, too, the range of knowledge and skills that a child can develop interacting with an adult or peer is greater than the child can gain alone (Vygotsky 1978).

Recently, the National Scientific Council on the Developing Child (2004) affirmed Vygotsky's theory: "Young children experience their world as an environment of relationships, and these relationships affect virtually all aspects of their development — intellectual, social, emotional, physical, behavioral, and moral" (p. 5).

Whether your interactions are spontaneous or planned, thoughtful or automatic, individualized or one-size-fits-all, the kind of interactions you have with children matters. The topic of teacher-child interactions has been very much in the forefront of the early childhood dialogue for several years. As you'll see throughout this book, there is extensive research to support the importance of enhancing the quality of interactions with children.

About This Book

Because your interactions make such a difference to children's development and learning, we hope this book will help you take a breath, step back, and take a careful look at how you interact with children.

For more than 30 years, we have talked and taught with other early childhood educators in various settings. Hearing from them about the challenges of getting to know each child as an individual led to our book *The Power of Observation* (1999/2007), which Judy and Amy wrote with our colleague and friend Margo Dichtelmiller. To help teachers make more meaningful connections between their observation and their teaching, Amy, Judy, and Charlotte wrote *Observation: The Key to Responsive Teaching* (2008).

This book, *Powerful Interactions: How to Connect with Children to Extend Their Learning,* takes the next step. Grounded in the reality of teachers' everyday lives and the research on effective teaching and child development, it shows you how to take what you know about children from observing them (and talking with their families) and use it to create an optimal opportunity for you to teach and the child to learn.

That opportunity is what we call a "Powerful Interaction."

We promise that transforming some of your everyday interactions into Powerful Interactions will deliver wonderful benefits for children — and *for you.* Children will become more engaged in exploring, thinking, and communicating. With this engagement will come greater motivation, which leads to greater learning. In turn, you will become more intentional and effective. You will feel (and be) more successful as a teacher! We believe that with these feelings of success, you'll gain the professional satisfaction of knowing the vital role you're playing in children's new accomplishments and growing sense of competence.

We have written and designed this book to become part of your daily practice. We hope you'll keep it flopped open on a countertop, and find something on every page each day to inspire you and make you smile, as you learn new strategies for your work with children. Throughout the book, we have included writing space where you can reflect on the new ideas and record your insights. Perhaps you'll join with other teachers in reading the book together, beginning a broader conversation about enhancing your teaching practice.

While this book will affirm what you already know and do well, we also invite you to learn some new ideas and skills, experiment with them, and share them with others. We're confident that in the process, you'll turn some of your everyday interactions into Powerful Interactions. ✳

Amy, Judy, and Charlotte
March 2011

POWERFUL INTERACTIONS: A FIRST LOOK

Interactions are the exchanges in words and gestures that you have with others — in particular, the exchanges that you as a teacher have with young children.

Each day and throughout the day you have dozens of interactions with children, in groups and one-on-one. There are times when you make comments, ask questions, provide information, or give instructions. At other times, you might acknowledge a child's effort, make requests, or correct something a child says. You may give hugs or pats on the back. You likely smile, frown, point, or wave. You interact when you greet children in the morning or say good-bye at the end of the day, during whole-group experiences and small-group activities, and as children work and play, both inside and outdoors. Even during transitions and daily routines you are interacting with children.

Giving your interactions some careful thinking is important because research shows that who you are, and how and what you say and do as you engage with children, makes a difference in what they learn about themselves, others, and the world (Hamre & Pianta 2005). This means that every one of your interactions holds the potential to make a positive impact on how children feel about themselves and about learning, as well as on what and how they learn.

Let's look at a few examples of the kinds of interactions that have a positive impact on children. Do you see yourself in any of these examples?

- Wilma greets Lucy and her grandfather in the morning, and with a smile on her face says, "Good morning, Lucy. We've been waiting for you so you can help us take a look inside this pomegranate." From her teacher, Lucy gets the message that she is an important and special person. She also hears the name of a new fruit that is fun to say.

- Robert asks 6-month-old Baili, "Are you ready for me to pick you up so we can change that wet diaper?" He waits for her to look at him and hold out her arms before reaching down. From this conversation, Baili learns about the give-and-take of communicating with another person. She also learns she can get her "I'm ready now" message across, and that Robert listens to her.

- Ms. Jackson sits beside 3-year-old Ryo on the couch in her family child care home. She listens to what he tells her about his picture of the fire engine, and she writes his words along the bottom edge of his drawing. From Ms. Jackson, Ryo is learning that the words he says can be written down and that his ideas are valuable enough to be recorded.

- Mr. Walden listens as 6-year-old Malika reads *Ten Apples Up On Top!* After a few pages, she says, "I can't read the rest yet." Mr. Walden grins at her and says, "I wish Dr. Seuss could hear you read this book! Maybe tomorrow, you and I can work on the next few pages together." Malika is reminded why she loves coming to school, and finds out that she won't be left to figure out the rest of the book alone.

Unfortunately, not all interactions children have with their teachers are so productive or positive. Some interactions send unintended messages that undermine children's confidence, take away the joy of exploration, and interfere with learning. Do you see yourself in any of these examples?

- When 2-year-old Fiona continually hears from her teacher, "Don't run," "No touching," and "Shhh," she gets the message that her excitement, curiosity, and language are not welcome.

- Running late, Ms. Smith dismisses Carla's question about bugs with a brusque, "Give me a minute!" From their quick exchange, Carla understands that her interest in bugs isn't important. She may become hesitant to ask questions. Later, during choice time, she sits quietly beside Damon at the computer rather than choosing her favorite area, the science center.

- Each day, as Joey waits for his turn to use the bathroom, his teacher tells him, "Just stand there in line quietly." Joey is learning that school is boring and that one way to make it more interesting is to fool around or start a fight.

- Ms. Annie sits beside Shantelle, who has just made a pattern using large blue bears and small orange bears. Ms. Annie says, "What color are the bears in your pattern?" Smiling, Shantelle responds blue and red. As Ms. Annie quizzes her in several different ways to get her to say orange, Shantelle's delight with her pattern fades, her smile disappears, and finally she pushes her chair away from the table.

Positive or negative, the quality and intentionality of your interactions with children matter. This is where Powerful Interactions come into play.

What Is a "Powerful Interaction"?

Teachers and children interact with each other all day long. Let's call these "everyday" interactions. In the typical classroom, most everyday interactions are perfectly fine — warm, caring, and encouraging. Sometimes they happen spontaneously, sometimes in a rush, often with little thought about a purpose. Children may or may not learn from them. Sometimes children learn what the teacher intends to teach, but other times they learn unintended lessons.

Not every interaction a teacher has with children can be — or even needs to be — an interaction that promotes their learning. But we might expect that many would have learning as the goal. This may sound a bit harsh, but research finds that interactions in which teachers *intentionally* promote learning are few and far between (Early et al. 2005; Pianta 2010).

At the other end of the continuum from everyday interactions are what we call "Powerful Interactions" — very intentional and purposeful exchanges between a teacher and a child that can have a significant and highly positive impact on learning.

In a Powerful Interaction, the teacher intentionally connects with a particular child in order to extend that child's learning.

You launch a Powerful Interaction when you make a conscious decision to say or do something that conveys to the child, "I notice you, I'm interested in you, and I want to know you better." This moment of personal connection builds upon the trust and security that exists between the two of you. Within a trusting and secure relationship, a child is more open to learn from the guidance and instruction you offer.

Let's watch as preschool teacher Ms. Pat has a Powerful Interaction with 3-year-old Jo-Jo.

Ms. Pat quickly checks the classroom to see how everyone is doing. Glancing over at the sand table, she sees Jo-Jo playing with a dump truck.

"Things are pretty calm here; the morning has gone smoothly so far. Jo-Jo is at the sand table by himself. This would be a good time to work one-on-one for a few minutes with Jo-Jo."

Ms. Pat goes to the sand table and kneels down to **connect** with Jo-Jo.

Ms. Pat: "Jo-Jo. I see you playing with the dump truck again. You play with this truck a lot. And I see you're using the shovel to fill it up with sand."

Jo-Jo looks up at Ms. Pat and smiles. He puts the shovel down and pushes the truck toward her. She smiles back at him.

"Mmmm. I've made a good connection. How can I use it to extend Jo-Jo's learning? I wonder if he can explain how dump trucks work?"

Ms. Pat: "You know so much about trucks, Jo-Jo. I saw a dump truck yesterday, and I have a question for you. Can you teach me how the dump truck works?"

Jo-Jo points to the lever on the side of the truck.

"He does know how dump trucks work, but he didn't use the word **lever**. I'll teach him the word."

Ms. Pat: "Oh! To dump the sand, you push the lever."

Jo-Jo: "Push a lever."

He takes her hand and puts it on the lever. They push down together, and the sand dumps out. They giggle.

Jo-Jo: "Push! ... Push more!"

Together they begin filling up the truck again.

How Do You Turn an Everyday Interaction into a Powerful Interaction?

In just a few minutes, Ms. Pat had a Powerful Interaction with Jo-Jo. Her interaction was a Powerful Interaction because she was deliberate about noticing the opportunity and preparing for the exchange. In order to make her teaching more effective and his learning meaningful, she connected with Jo-Jo to activate and deepen her relationship with him by sharing his interest in trucks, and she intentionally extended Jo-Jo's learning by introducing a new and interesting word.

Like Ms. Pat, you can make what could have been just another everyday interaction ("Just 5 more minutes in the sandbox, Jo-Jo!") a Powerful Interaction. A Powerful Interaction has three steps.

Step One — Be Present

When you are "present" you are in the moment and self-aware, and therefore you can be more open to the interesting and significant things that children do. By physically and mentally slowing down for just a few moments, you can pay better attention. This frame of mind allows you to be *intentional*; that is, before you act, to tune in to what a child is doing at that moment, how you are feeling, and what you want to accomplish. Being intentional in this way means you think about what to say and do in the interaction to be most effective as a teacher for that child.

Because Ms. Pat was alert to what all the children were doing, she observed Jo-Jo in the sandbox. She took a second to collect her thoughts before joining him for a Powerful Interaction.

Step Two — Connect

You acknowledge and validate children by letting them know you see them, are interested in them, and want to spend time with them. Connecting in this way awakens the sense of trust and security that previous positive interactions between you and the child are helping to develop. As your relationships with children grow deeper, children feel more confident and focused, and they are more open to learning from you.

Positive relationships, like the one evident between Ms. Pat and Jo-Jo, lay the foundation for children's exploration and learning. Positive relationships also enhance the likelihood of children's engagement and achievement in school (Center for Social and Emotional Education n.d.; Gallagher & Mayer 2008; Howes & Ritchie 2002).

The smile Jo-Jo gave Ms. Pat when she approached him was evidence that they had connected and were building on an already positive relationship. Ms. Pat reinforced that relationship by joining Jo-Jo in what he was already doing, kneeling beside him, showing interest in his play, and acknowledging his expertise with dump trucks.

Step Three — Extend Learning

When you extend a child's knowledge and understanding hand-in-hand with nurturing a positive relationship with that child, you create the optimal condition for you to teach and the child to learn (Birch & Ladd 1997). During the fertile minutes of a Powerful Interaction, children are open to your adding to their knowledge, encouraging them to try new things and think in new ways, modeling language, introducing interesting new vocabulary, and other learning possibilities.

To extend Jo-Jo's learning, Ms. Pat decided to ask a question that invited the child to consolidate and share his knowledge ("Can you teach me how the dump truck works?") and then she introduced him to the word *lever* ("To dump the sand, you push the lever").

A Cumulative Effect

Often when we think about steps in a process, we think about them coming sequentially — first, then second, then third. Instead, these three Powerful Interaction steps are cumulative — they build on one another. You begin with Step One by stopping for a moment to **be present.** In this inward frame of mind, you can decide to *add* Step Two, choosing what to say and do to **connect** with the child. Staying present and connected, you then *add* Step Three, as you select and apply a teaching strategy to **extend the child's learning.**

In this book, we describe the three steps separately and in detail to help you understand the importance of each one. Once you have practiced and are more comfortable having Powerful Interactions with children, each step will flow naturally from the previous one. Each would be visible as separate from the others only if you were able to watch an instant replay of yourself in slow motion. (In fact, we'll return to this useful idea of instant replay in the last chapter, "Powerful Interactions: You Make the Difference!")

In real life, as a Powerful Interaction unfolds, the three steps are apt to happen very quickly. The whole of Ms. Pat's Powerful Interaction with Jo-Jo, for example, might have lasted just a minute or two, from her seeing him at the sand table to his repeating the new word, *lever*.

What's in It for You?

Clearly, Powerful Interactions deliver wonderful benefits for children. You'll find that children thrive from having deeper relationships with you. Their confidence will build, their engagement and motivation will increase, and as a result, they'll become more successful learners.

We trust, too, that you will come to see the positive effect Powerful Interactions can have on you! Transforming just some of your everyday interactions with children into Powerful Interactions will make your teaching more effective and your work more rewarding. Here are some benefits to look forward to:

● **Your interactions with children will become more intentional.**

Practicing the three steps of Powerful Interactions (Be Present, Connect, Extend Learning) helps you make more intentional decisions about what to say and do. In a Powerful Interaction, you are thoughtful and alert, paying attention to yourself, your emotions, your actions, and your words. You draw upon your knowledge both of individual children and of how children typically develop; and you learn to respond deliberately, rather than react. Thus, you can more effectively support children's learning, because you are able to anticipate your impact on the child and the child's impact on you.

Since you introduced me to Powerful Interactions, my assistant and I find that we are teaching with intent rather than on autopilot. The result is that we have a greater understanding of each individual child's development and can respond in ways that are appropriate for that child.

— Corrine (a preschool teacher)

● **Your instruction will become more individualized.**

In a Powerful Interaction, you are focused on that child. You're observing what the child is doing, and you're making instructional decisions that fit the child's need right in that moment. As the Powerful Interaction evolves, you can see whether your guidance is effective; and if not, you immediately can adjust accordingly — use a different word, offer a new challenge, help the child make a link, or offer a different material. You're individualizing instruction in a highly effective way.

> *"[Intentional teachers] have a repertoire of instructional strategies and know when to use a given strategy to accommodate the different ways that individual children learn and the specific content they are learning."*
>
> *— Epstein 2007, 1*

● **The climate in your classroom will improve.**

Through Powerful Interactions, your relationships with children grow stronger. These positive relationships set an example for children to follow, and their peer relationships improve, as well. In this environment, children are calmer, behavior problems are reduced, and more time can be devoted to learning (Meyers & Morris 2009; Phillips et al. 1987; Vick Whittaker & Jones Harden 2010).

> *My classroom is more relaxed and children are competing less for my attention. My interactions with them seem to satisfy them more now because I'm so much more attentive when I'm with them. I'm really talking with them rather than just giving them the "Good jobs."*
>
> *— Darice (a preschool teacher)*

- **Your partnerships with families will grow.**

  Powerful Interactions allow you to observe children making discoveries and practicing new skills. You have wonderful, individualized, specific stories to share with family members, which bring you closer together.

- **Your teaching practice will grow richer and become more enjoyable.**

  Powerful Interactions energize you and your teaching. As you learn to quiet the mental static that keeps you from being present, you give yourself the gift of truly seeing and being with a child. As children gradually reveal their individual interests and personalities to you, your Powerful Interactions with them are moments to remember. Over time, as you develop the Powerful Interactions habit, these moments, and the feelings of joy and pride they bring, are more and more frequent.

  > *When I consciously knew that my goal was to have Powerful Interactions with just four children each day, I could relax and not feel rushed.*
  >
  > *My first happened during Morning Centers, and I found myself enjoying — I mean REALLY enjoying — that child. I felt that same excitement when interacting with the others that day, and I ended up giving hugs.*
  >
  > *I think the children see my joy and that I truly value our conversations, and they seem to open up and offer more than before. … I look forward to each day and can't wait to sit down to talk with children to see what I can learn from them and about them.*
  >
  > *— Darlene (a preschool teacher)*

As you explore this book, you'll find all the information you need to begin transforming everyday interactions with children into Powerful Interactions. You'll discover strategies to use to **be present, connect,** and **extend children's learning.** Some may seem familiar and reinforce what you're already doing; some strategies will be new and can take your teaching in exciting new directions.

Within these pages you'll also read many stories of teachers already using Powerful Interactions to individualize their instruction to each child's interests, needs, and abilities. Like them, you'll soon realize that using Powerful Interactions helps you make a positive difference in the lives of children and their families … which, in turn, will make a positive difference in your life as a teacher.

We think you'll enjoy the process!

STEP ONE:
BE PRESENT

Slow down for a moment so you can
be intentional in your interaction

STEP TWO: STEP THREE:
CONNECT   EXTEND
                   LEARNING

STEP ONE:
BE PRESENT

As you read this chapter, pause to reflect on what you're learning. How could you use its ideas and strategies in your setting?

STEP ONE:
BE PRESENT

Ever feel like there's so much going on in your mind you can barely hear yourself think? We call this mental noise *static*. It's like the annoying crackling sound on your phone that makes it hard to have a conversation, or the distracting commercials that interrupt your favorite TV show — except the static is in your head. When you're trying to focus, static can drive you crazy!

Static affects us all. It's everywhere — at home and in the classroom — whenever too many people and too many things demand our attention *now*! Early childhood settings can be busy, noisy, active places where you have to juggle many tasks and priorities at once. It's no wonder the static in your head can become so loud that many of your everyday interactions with children happen without much thought about what you are going to say and do and why.

Taking the first step toward turning some of your everyday interactions into Powerful Interactions requires quieting the static. Static interferes with having a Powerful Interaction because the mental distraction makes it difficult for you to think clearly. When there's static, it's difficult to remember and draw upon the personal qualities and experience you bring to your teaching, your knowledge of the individual children in your group, and what you know about how children typically develop and learn. Static gets in the way of knowing how you're feeling. It's difficult to focus. Static makes it hard to be present.

What Does It Mean to "Be Present"?

To have a Powerful Interaction, whether it lasts one minute or five, your first step is to be present. To **be present** means pausing for just a moment to quiet your static and prepare to join the child in the interaction. With a quieter mind, you can think. You can focus. You can decide how to respond with intention rather than simply react. Pausing to be present puts you in a clear and open frame of mind so that you can be intentional in a Powerful Interaction.

WHAT CAUSES STATIC FOR YOU?

Being present means quieting your static. You allow yourself to be fully in the moment. You are focused not on what you were doing a second ago or what you need to do tomorrow. You're thinking only about the now. When you quiet the static, you let go of feelings that may interfere with clear thinking. Are you still aggravated about what happened at breakfast that morning? Are you worried about the parent conference later today? How you're feeling affects what you will say and do in the interaction. Remember, what you say and do as you interact affects how children feel about themselves and about learning (Hamre & Pianta 2005). Clearing your mind of static allows you to focus on the child and give him your full attention. You're more in control of your words and actions.

Being present means taking a moment to think and prepare. When you can think clearly, you can tap into the knowledge you have about yourself and the child and figure out how to make the interaction a success. A Powerful Interaction requires chemistry: a "just-right" fit between you and the child. What's worked well in previous interactions with this child? What may have gotten in the way? Does this child push your buttons? Perhaps you have come to know that there's something about who you are that makes it hard for you to get along with him. The more honest you can be with yourself, the more effective you will be as you interact with children.

You might be wondering, why is it so important to be present? Young children have an uncanny ability to tune in to the important adults in their life. They can read the meaning behind the sound of your voice, your facial expressions, how you hold yourself and move. They know when you're being genuine and when you're not. They know when you are irritable or distracted and when you are right there with them. You can't fool them! That is why "*how* you are with children is as important as what you *do*" (Pawl & St. John 1998, 3).

When you are focused and aware of your feelings, you can be more *intentional* about your words and actions. You're more prepared to speak and act in ways that will be most effective as a teacher for that child at that moment. As a result, you're better able to make intentional decisions in the second and third steps of a Powerful Interaction (**Connect** and **Extend Learning**).

Let's watch Julia, a kindergarten teacher, as she pauses to be present and prepare for a Powerful Interaction:

> It's center time in Julia's classroom. Her mind is racing with everything she's done in the last 30 minutes: making sure the children have materials, managing flow, and getting everyone settled into activities. As she moves about the room, she notices 5-year-old Hakeem working on a puzzle.
>
> She pauses for a few seconds, thinking to herself: "Whew! I've been on autopilot. To connect with Hakeem, I need to pause and get on his wavelength. When I do puzzles, I'm all about finishing; Hakeem studies every single piece. I know I tend to get impatient. Can I be more patient with his style so that together we can have a Powerful Interaction?" Julia takes a deep breath, relaxes her face, and settles her shoulders. "Sure, I can do it." With that, she walks over to sit beside Hakeem.

Julia quieted her mind, thought about herself, thought about Hakeem, and then decided she was ready to have a Powerful Interaction.

As you can see, being present is vital to having a Powerful Interaction. Now let's think about what it takes to actually become present.

Doing a Quick "Me Check"

To be present and prepare for a Powerful Interaction, you stop and breathe for a moment. You pause to consider two questions:

Can I quiet the static? In the above vignette, Julia realizes that she's been on autopilot. Her mind is racing and full of mental noise. Just pausing for a second to think about how she feels calms her mind and reduces some of the static.

Do I need to adjust to connect with this child, and if so, how? Julia recalls past interactions with Hakeem. She knows that their different styles can clash and that her impatience with his methodical way of working can show in her body and tone of voice, and therefore can undermine her effectiveness with him. She knows that as the adult and teacher, she's the one who has to let go of her impatience toward Hakeem and modify her way of being with him if she wants to have a Powerful Interaction!

Asking yourself these two questions is what we call doing a "Me Check." By first quieting the static, you can think clearly. Then, you can reflect on what you know about the child and about yourself. You can make more deliberate decisions about how to respond to what the child needs, rather than just react to the child's behavior or personality or your own needs. Once you get the hang of it, a Me Check takes less than a minute.

Taking a deeper look at each of the Me Check questions will help you understand and use them more effectively.

Me Check — "Can I quiet the static?"

At the beginning of this chapter, you identified some of the factors that cause static for you. Your level of static is likely to change throughout the day. Sometimes the static is really loud. Other times it's less. One moment, your static level may be low because you're relaxed and delighted when a child tells you a silly joke. Or perhaps you are excited to try a new activity with the children. At another time, your static level is high because you're tense and tired and then you have to remind Danny yet again that the fish are fed only once a day.

Here's how some teachers tell us they quiet the static:

- *I take some deep breaths and look outside the window.*
- *I imagine I'm putting everything that's on my mind in a to-do list so that I can focus solely on the child.*
- *I picture a "static meter" in my mind. If it registers high, I know I have to make an extra effort to quiet down — and I do.*
- *My teaching partner and I check in with each other during the day on our static levels. Yesterday when hers was high, I suggested she take a walk outside with a few children. It helped her; and when she was quieter inside, so was I.*

DID YOU KNOW?

Emotional intelligence is the ability to tune in to your own emotions and the emotions of other people. Having emotional intelligence helps you know which of your emotions will help support the child you are trying to reach, and which emotions to set aside (e.g., your tension about not having forms ready for your director or your anger at your spouse).

Sometimes your static is just too great. Perhaps there's so much going on in the room or in your life that it's asking too much of yourself to quiet your mind right now. Deciding not to have a Powerful Interaction in this moment can be an excellent intentional decision. Other times, however, you may need to make a conscious effort to put aside factors that interfere with being present. It isn't always easy, but it is a part of being a teaching professional.

Being aware of how loud your static is and where it's coming from can help you more easily quiet your mind. This in turn lets you be present so that Powerful Interactions become possible.

Me Check — "Do I need to adjust to connect with this child, and if so, how?"

The second Me Check question involves reflecting on your personal qualities and those of the child — your temperaments, preferences and interests, cultures and language. Reflect on your past interactions together. What's worked well? What hasn't worked? What have you done in the past to complement the child's way of being? Will some little adjustments in how you act be necessary to create a just-right fit and have an enjoyable and productive interaction this time?

As adults, we often make mental adjustments to fit with our family members, friends, and colleagues, sometimes without noticing we are doing so. For example, when your spouse arrives home at the end of the day and you sense he or she is upset, you may decide to be a little less talkative than you typically are. You may decide to quiet your own excitement from having had a great day and make your greeting a little quieter and less wordy. Or when your daughter runs over to show you the stickers she is so thrilled to be collecting, you smile and share her pleasure even though you find them pretty uninteresting.

When we interact with other adults, we expect that the other person can and will assume some of the responsibility and adjust to us, too. Ideally, both adults are able to shift the way they act and what they say and do in order to connect with each other. Of course, there will be times when one person will do more adjusting than the other, but that's part of the give-and-take of interacting productively with others.

When you interact with a child, however, it is up to you as the teacher to take the lead and adjust to the child, if you want to have a Powerful Interaction. It is helpful to think about ways that you and individual children may differ. Let's look at some of them.

Temperament. Temperament is a person's nature and affects behavior. Some people refer to temperament as a person's "way of being." Your temperament is a core part of who you are. Sometimes your temperament meshes really well with a child's. Other times, temperaments don't mesh well and can get in the way of a Powerful Interaction.

To prepare for a Powerful Interaction, Rema reflects on how her temperament differs from Ryan's:

> Rema is about to join 5-year-old Ryan in the writing center. After quieting her mental static, she recalls prior interactions with Ryan. She thinks, "My structured, organized style is totally unlike Ryan's. He can suddenly pop up out of his seat and rush over to the library area to look for a picture in a book. One minute he's using markers. The next minute, he's switched to colored pencils.
>
> "I tend to think of him as unfocused and inattentive, even misbehaving. But that's just his temperament. And it's different from mine — not better or worse, just different. I need to remember that Ryan's just being himself. He shouldn't have to act like me for me to relate to him. I can be more accepting of his temperament, appreciative of his efforts, and even smile a little bit to help us connect."

 Temperament — How would you describe your own temperament? The temperaments of specific children in your program? What are some ways you have to adjust for a just-right fit?

All of us are born with our own style of interacting with people, places, objects, and situations. Although none of us fits neatly into a box or responds in the same way all the time, researchers have identified three basic types of temperament. Which are you?

- Easygoing or flexible
- Slow to warm or cautious
- Intense or feisty

Preferences and interests. Your personal preferences and interests can affect your reactions to children, as well as your willingness to join them in their work and play. The more you understand yourself — your likes and dislikes — the more flexible you can be as you connect with a child. Notice how Iris uses the Me Check to find a way to mesh with Luisa:

> Before joining 4-year-old Luisa in the dramatic play area, Iris takes a moment to quiet the static and be present. She thinks, "Wow. I haven't had a Powerful Interaction with Luisa in a few days. I bet it's because she always chooses dramatic play and that's not an area where I like to spend time. But I know that dramatic play is a perfect place to extend her language, so I just need to put my mind to it and go over there."

Are there things children in your program are interested in that you don't enjoy, making it a challenge to interact with them? Perhaps there's a child in your program who loves insects, but you get squeamish when she brings you the ones she finds on the playground. If you could let go of your discomfort and share her interest, you might be able to have a Powerful Interaction and extend her learning. Just as Iris did, you may have to push yourself and be a little flexible in order to make a connection.

Interests and Preferences — Do you see yourself in Iris's story? Are there things children in your program like to do that you don't enjoy, making a just-right fit challenging?

Culture and language. Each of us has a set of beliefs about ourselves, as well as attitudes, assumptions, and expectations about other people and the world around us — some that we may not even be aware of. These beliefs and attitudes come to us from the way we were raised, our family and community, our class and background. They are our *culture*. Combined with our temperament and our preferences and interests, culture helps make us who we are.

Our culture is reflected in how we communicate with, judge, and respond to others. When people come from different cultures, they may not always view the world, society, and people the same way. But to build a relationship, we have to find something inside us or the other person that will be a starting place for a positive connection. In this next example, Ms. D grapples with how her cultural beliefs might interfere with her interaction with a child:

DID YOU KNOW?

Ever hear the expression "walk a mile in my shoes" or "see the world through her eyes"? This is called *perspective taking* — an essential life skill that children need in order to be successful adults (Galinsky 2010).

Early childhood experts are studying how important this skill of perspective taking is for teachers to have in order to be effective. It is also important that teachers model the skill for children. After you pause to be present and do a Me Check, you are prepared to see children's experiences through their eyes.

Ms. D, a first grade teacher, has noticed Elizabeth at the easel painting a picture that includes religious symbols. She has paused to quiet her static and is thinking about adjustments she might have to make to connect positively with Elizabeth. She calls up past interactions with Elizabeth and thinks, "Her artwork is often about religion, and she's eager to share her family's beliefs. I get a bit uncomfortable because my family background is so different. It makes it hard for me to connect with her. I guess I'm having trouble being accepting of our differences.

"This time I'm going to let go of my worries and judgments, and begin this interaction with an open mind. I'm going to listen to her description of her painting, encourage her to write about it, and stay open to what I'm learning about her."

In these examples, Rema, Iris, and Ms. D acknowledged the ways they didn't quite mesh with each child. The second Me Check question requires that you consider what you know about the child from previous interactions and how you might have to adjust in order to make a Powerful Interaction with that child possible. When interacting with children, the adult is the one responsible for making a just-right fit. If a Powerful Interaction is to succeed, your insight and willingness to do the adjusting are musts.

Culture and Language — Can you recall a time when your language, background, or attitudes helped you connect with a child? When it may have interfered?

Getting Better at "Being Present"

If it seems like we're asking a lot of you during this quick moment before interacting with children, we are. But we think it's worth it, because Powerful Interactions will make such a positive difference. Powerful Interactions will strengthen your relationships with children, which in turn make children more open to your teaching. They'll learn more and feel better about themselves as learners. For you, Powerful Interactions are going to make your teaching more effective, which in turn can lead to your feeling better about yourself and your work.

Here are a few ideas to try that can help you get better at being present. Some work right in the moment. Others may take some practice or need to be done at another time:

Take a few deep breaths. Sometimes this is the best way to quiet the static and start being present.

Do a quick body scan. Where in your body are you holding tension or other negative emotions? Your shoulders? Neck? Jaw? See if you can let the tension go. A quick stretch may help.

Use your "real" voice. Even the youngest children can sense when you are not giving them your undivided attention or being genuine about your feelings. Instead of using your "teacher" voice, focus on the child as an individual and have a conversation together.

Arrange your setting to feel comfortable and affirming. Be sure there are comfy places for you to sit and be with adults and children. If you like flowers, bring a flower for yourself each week and display it on your counter.

Share with a trusted friend or colleague. Talk about doing the Me Check and discuss different ways you might answer its two questions. Reflect on ways you might have to adjust your attitude, behavior, and thinking in order to connect positively with some of the children in your program.

REALITY CHECK It's impossible to be positive and engaged with every child in your program all the time. Doing a Me Check before deciding whether to launch a Powerful Interaction gives you a moment to slow down, recognize issues that might get in the way of being genuine with children, and ask yourself, "Can I put them aside for a few minutes?" If your answer is no too often, that may tell you something about yourself that's worth exploring further.

You'll know that you are starting to be present more often when

- You are more aware of static in your daily life and how it can interfere with your ability to see and think clearly.

- You're beginning to do Me Checks and noticing how paying attention to your state of mind helps you make more intentional decisions throughout the day.

- You take time to think about what you bring to your teaching and how what's inside you can affect your decisions about what to say and do in your interactions with children and families.

You'll know that being present is becoming a habit when

- You feel yourself putting aside distracting feelings or thoughts — and your cell phone — that interfere with your really seeing and being there with children. (You can always come back to your issues during your lunch hour, at break, or at the end of the day.)

- Your setting feels more relaxed and comfortable and is filled with positive energy.

- You can admit to yourself that a particular child or family member pushes your buttons (no one likes everyone all of the time). Yet, you still are able to connect, building a foundation for the positive relationship needed to work effectively with them.

Finally, you'll know that you are really good at being present when

- You begin an interaction with a child, realize it isn't going well, and pause to do a Me Check in order to be present and try again.

Powerful Interactions begin with you. The more you know yourself, the more effective you can be with children. Powerful Interactions are intentional. The first step of a Powerful Interaction — **Be Present** — allows you to think and prepare. By pausing to be present before interacting, you can make deliberate decisions about what you do and say in Steps Two and Three.

Now let's look at Step Two. **Connect** is about making and sustaining personal connections with children to deepen your relationships with them and make them more open to learning from you. *

STEP TWO: CONNECT

Acknowledge and validate the child
to awaken the trust and security
developing between you

STEP ONE:
BE PRESENT

STEP THREE:
EXTEND
LEARNING

STEP TWO:
CONNECT

As you read this chapter, pause to reflect on what you're learning. How could you use its ideas and strategies in your setting?

STEP TWO: CONNECT

You have taken the first step, **Be Present.** This means you're fully in the moment — in control of your thoughts and feelings and focused on the child. You have given some thought to the just-right fit — what you know about the child's and your temperament, preferences and interests, and culture and language, and you have considered whether or not you might need to adjust to make the interaction work well. In this frame of mind, you can be intentional, choosing what to say and do to both build a relationship with and be most effective as a teacher for that child at that moment.

You're ready to add Step Two — to connect with the child and launch a Powerful Interaction. Staying calm and open, you approach the child, tapping into the trust and security that exists between the two of you. Within a trusting and secure relationship, a child is more open to learn from the guidance and instruction you will offer in Step Three, **Extend Learning.** Also, each positive interaction you have further deepens your relationship, which helps the child feel even more safe, confident, and ready to learn.

What Does It Mean to "Connect"?

Connecting means observing what is interesting and significant about what the child is doing, saying, and thinking. It means letting the child know that you see her, are interested in what she is doing, and want to spend some time with her. Watch as these teachers approach and connect with children.

Notice what each teacher does and says to connect:

As Ms. Zora joins 2-year-old Dennis at the sandbox, she initiates a connection with him by giving him a warm smile. She says, "Hi, Dennis! I've been watching you digging this great big hole. Your muscles are getting such a workout!" Dennis looks up at Ms. Zora with a huge grin on his face. Opening his eyes wide, he says to her, "Big hole!"

Three-year-old Celia has dumped a basket of smooth stones on the rug and is putting them back in one by one, saying a number in random order each time. Mr. Yosef settles in next to her on the floor and, leaning in toward her just a little bit, comments: "I heard all these numbers and wondered who was practicing their counting. It's Celia!" She says, "Wanna watch me?"

Slowly and methodically, 4-year-old Khalid looks through every book on the bookshelf. Mr. Hall watches him and decides to initiate a Powerful Interaction. He silently kneels beside him and joins in his search for a good book. After a few seconds, Khalid takes one of the books off the shelf, holds it in his lap, and begins turning the pages slowly. Mr. Hall does the same. Sitting quietly beside Khalid, Mr. Hall watches to see the child's body settle and senses that he is getting comfortable with the teacher's presence before beginning to talk about the book.

Relationships and Learning

Connecting with a child as you begin a Powerful Interaction acts as a reminder to that child of the relationship you share together. And with that reminder comes the comfortable and reassuring feelings of security, confidence, and competence.

In turn, these feelings of security, confidence, and competence free children to take risks, experiment, explore, discover, and stretch their skills and thinking. This link between emotional safety and learning has been identified and described by researchers, who tell us that the quality of teacher-child relationships influences children's achievement in school (National Research Council 2001).

As John Bowlby's work on attachment revealed many years ago, successful learning requires that a child develop meaningful early relationships (Bowlby 1969). Today, thanks to advances in technology and science, we know that when you and the other important adults in children's lives pay attention to their emotional and social needs, as well as to their learning, you actually help shape the architecture of their brains, which opens the door for the future mastery of literacy and cognitive skills (National Scientific Council on the Developing Child 2007).

We sometimes talk about building relationships with children as if it were a task that can be completed and checked off a to-do list, freeing us to turn our attention to our "real" job of teaching. However, relationships with young

RELATIONSHIPS MATTER

- When teachers establish emotionally secure relationships with children, these relationships contribute to children's engagement in school. (Morrison 2007)

- In elementary school, children's descriptions of their relationships with their teachers predict children's coping behavior, feelings of autonomy, and engagement in school. (Furrer & Skinner 2003)

- Teacher's reported closeness to individual children predicts children's academic success. (Pianta 2000)

- If teachers show more positive emotion and sensitivity, and are less harsh and detached, young children are more likely to be engaged in the classroom. (Ridley et al. 2000)

Adapted with permission from *Enthusiastic and Engaged Learners: Approaches to Learning in the Early Childhood Classroom*. 2008. Marilou Hyson, New York: Teachers College Press; and Washington, DC: NAEYC.

children are never "done." They are ongoing, evolving with every encounter. Every interaction we have with a child holds the potential to make a positive — or negative — impact on how that child feels about himself and about learning, as well as on what and how the child learns.

Individualize Your Connections

Deciding how to connect with a child at the beginning of a Powerful Interaction depends on what you know about that child. Think back to the Me Check in the previous chapter. The second Me Check question ("Do I need to adjust to connect with this child, and if so, how?") prompts you to use what you have learned about the child to anticipate adjustments you might have to make to fit with that child.

To begin the interaction, you observe the child with an open mind and adjust your pace, energy level, patience, and approach in ways that complement the child's temperament, preferences and interests, culture and language, and behavior. This is the way you ensure that the child continues to feel comfortable with and respected by you.

Each time you invite a connection, you'll need to be alert to how the child responds. How you go about connecting with children also may need to shift as they grow and change, each in his or her own unique way. For example, an energetic, enthusiastic child typically might require you to perk up a bit to match her excitement. Yet, in a different situation the same child might need you to be calmer or slower in order to help her settle down.

Children have many different ways of letting you know that you have connected and that they're ready to join you in learning. Children's temperament, level of comfort, and age and stage of development all influence what clues they offer. Over time, a child's clues may change as your relationship grows and as the child develops greater confidence and social skills. The obvious clues (e.g., smiling) are easiest to recognize. Gradually, as your observation skills become sharper, you'll start to recognize the more subtle ones.

To signal a connection and a willingness to join you in learning, a child may

- Look at you and smile
- Reach out to be picked up
- Continue playing, but with a little extra focus and enthusiasm
- Involve you in her play
- Show or tell you something
- Ask you a question

Once your offer to connect has been accepted by the child and a connection is made, your aim is to maintain the connection throughout the interaction. Monitor your body language, tone of voice, and the expression on your face so that the child continues to feel safe and secure with you. As you maintain the connection, observe the child so that you can decide how best to extend her learning, which we'll explore in Step Three.

 Connection Signals — For each child in your group, ask yourself what the child does or says to let you know you've connected. What new or different signals would you add to the list above?

Respecting a Rejection

Sometimes a child's response to your invitation will be, "No thanks … not now." He may use words or gestures to communicate this, or he may simply ignore you. He may be telling you he wants or needs to work alone right then. Or perhaps he doesn't yet feel comfortable enough with you. Don't take it personally or press your agenda too aggressively. Use patience and gentle persistence to gain the child's confidence, comfort, and trust. There will be other times you can connect and deepen your relationship with the child.

Watch how this teacher shows respect for a child's response:

> Margaret observes Nigal at the computer, does a Me Check, and decides to join him. Nigal doesn't look up. Margaret says, "Nigal, I notice that you're using the drawing program on the computer." No response from Nigal. Sensing that perhaps Nigal is choosing to ignore her, and wanting to show him respect, Margaret asks, "Nigal, would you prefer to work alone now?" Nigal nods his head. Placing her hand gently on his shoulder, Margaret says, "I appreciate that. I'll stop by later and see how you're doing. Enjoy your quiet work time."
>
> About 10 minutes later Margaret returns. This time Nigal looks up at her. Margaret comments, "I see that you have added so many colors to your drawing."

Margaret knows that Nigal is cautious about adults and slow to warm. She is patient yet gently persistent in her effort to help Nigal trust her. To nurture your relationship, be sensitive to the child's cues, whatever they are. Trust builds when children see that you are respectful of their needs.

Think of a recent connection you made with a child you work with. How did you know that your invitation to connect had been accepted? What did the child do or say that let you know a connection had been made? Now think about a connection you made with another child; what did that child say or do?

Seven Strategies for Connecting

In the pages that follow, you'll learn about seven strategies that you can use to connect with children and nurture the positive relationships you are building, so that each child will be open to learn from your guidance and instruction.

We describe each strategy separately so that you can understand and think about each one carefully. In reality, you'll likely use the strategies in conjunction with one another. For example, when you listen, you also show respect for and learn about children. When you guide them to behave in positive ways, you're also keeping the trust between you growing.

Each of the seven strategies described below is designed to help you connect with children to nurture your relationships and add to your effectiveness as a teacher.

1. **Slow Down, Stay in the Moment.** When you show children that you are interested in them and that you want to be with them, they can relax and be in the moment with you. Slowing down also gives you time to really tune in to and enjoy being with that child.

2. **Keep Learning about Children.** When you show children your genuine interest in them and willingness to learn more about them, they are more likely to connect with you and reveal more about themselves. You, in turn, will get to know children extremely well and see the unique wonder of each one.

3. **Listen to Children.** When you show children that you are actively listening to them, they are more likely to share who they really are with you. You will grow to appreciate each child as an individual. Your relationship with each child will grow deeper and stronger.

4. **Personalize Your Interactions.** Responding to children as unique individuals allows you to build a genuine connection that gives each child a solid base from which to move out into the world, explore, and learn. Observing children closely and customizing your responses to them allows you the joy of seeing the world through a child's eyes.

5. **Show Respect.** When you respect children, it shapes everything you say and do. When children experience your respect, they feel stronger, more confident and competent, and more trusting of you. Consequently, they will be more inclined to cooperate with you.

6. **Guide Children's Behavior.** When you convey to children that you are on their team, helping them behave in positive ways, they sense that you care and are there for them. Your relationship strengthens. You will find it easier to manage challenging behaviors as they arise.

7. **Keep Trust Growing.** As the trust between you continues to develop, children know they can count on you. This allows them to feel comfortable to explore and experiment — prerequisites to taking full advantage of learning opportunities throughout the day. The trust between you affirms the vital role you play in children's life and learning.

As you connect with children, the time you spend together throughout each day will become more rewarding and filled with learning for all of you.

Now let's explore the seven strategies for Step Two, **Connect.** ✳

Slow Down,
Stay in the Moment

Imagine you are in a place that you love. You've slowed down so that you can just *be there*. You are tuned in to the sights, sounds, smells … every little detail of the experience.

Tune out distractions and tune in to one child and what that child is doing.

- If it's the ocean you love, you might see crystal blue water with foamy whitecaps, hear waves rolling up to the shore, and smell the crisp salt air.

- Maybe you're in the city. You see sidewalks filled with people and pots of flowers in front of a *bodega*. You hear car horns, and smell the tangy barbeque from the cart on the corner.

- Or are you in the comfy chair in your living room? You see your child playing dress-up on the rug in front of you. You hear your favorite music, and smell the spicy curry that's simmering on the stove.

When you slow down and really tune in to what's happening around you, you get a complete view of things. In a similar way, slowing down to connect with a child allows you to be open to all the child is showing you right now.

Stay in the Moment to Connect with Children

When you decide to slow down and stay in the moment, it may look like you're doing nothing. It may even feel at first like you're doing nothing. But that's not true.

Slowing down allows you to really focus on a child and make a personal connection with him. Think of your attention to a child as a soft white light that encircles him. The child senses your interest, relaxes, and begins to trust that you'll be there. As you connect with him, your relationship deepens. Your calm attention to the child helps you to really see him, and at the same time allows him to focus on what he is doing and thinking. He becomes more open to learning with you.

In this example, notice how Sandra, a family child care provider, stays in the moment and connects with 3-year-old Louis, enhancing their relationship and setting the stage for his learning.

> Sandra has been busy getting children up from their naps. But now she slows down to do a quick Me Check and decides to initiate a Powerful Interaction with Louis. She sits down at the table with him. She quietly watches with a smile on her face as he pokes green playdough with his finger. After a few moments, she puts a cookie cutter on the table beside him.

From Sandra's quiet attention, Louis may be feeling any of the following:

- "She likes me."
- "She pays attention to me."
- "She thinks I'm important."
- "She cares about what I am doing."
- "I was going to get up, but I think I'll sit here a little longer."
- "I wonder what I can do with this cookie cutter."

REALITY

CHECK

You may worry that when you sit quietly beside a child, other adults may think you're not doing your job. Talking with colleagues about the importance of slowing down and staying in the moment can help them understand what you're doing.

Tips for Slowing Down and Staying in the Moment

As you begin an interaction, it can be challenging to proceed slowly and stay in the moment so that you can observe and connect. You'll have to find the way that works best for you. Here are some ideas:

Find a way to be comfortable so you can spend more time sitting at the child's level. Try a floor cushion. A low stool. A low folding chair. A milk crate with a pillow.

Take a deep breath and count to 10 as you join the child, to help yourself quiet down and observe.

Coordinate with your teaching partner. Be sure one of you is keeping an eye on the whole room so the other can focus on a few individual children.

How's It Going?

It's sometimes hard to slow down and connect in a Powerful Interaction. It will take practice. As you get better at slowing down and staying in the moment, look for clues that your efforts are making a difference in what is happening around you.

You may notice that

- Children seem more relaxed and comfortable with you as your relationship deepens

- You have more detailed stories to share with families about their children, and they in turn share more stories with you

- You are getting to know children better, because you're more patient and willing to let them show you what they know and can do at their own pace

- You are using this strategy more often to connect with others — in your teaching practice and in your personal life

REALITY

You can't always slow down. There will always be times you have to be busy to keep children safe and the day rolling.

CHECK

- Your space has more comfortable places to be seated at a child's level, leading you to sit with and connect with children more often

- Your program's overall climate is calmer, because everyone is slowing down and connecting with each other

Remember: *When you slow down and stay in the moment, it may not look like much is happening. But you are connecting with children, which strengthens your relationship with them—and this helps them to be more effective learners.*

Keep Learning
about Children

Imagine your phone rings, and your good friend asks, "How are you? What happened at school today?"

Open your eyes and mind to notice the interesting and significant things a child is showing you.

- She cares about you and wants to know how you're doing.

- She's open to what you have to say. You feel her curiosity and interest as she asks you questions and invites you to say more.

- Today is a new day, different from yesterday, and she appreciates that what you did and how you feel today may be different, too.

- She's with you, tuned in and listening.

- You feel like you have all the time you need to share your story.

How does it feel when someone — like this friend — is open to what you're saying and wants to keep learning about you?

Use What You Learn to Connect

As you join a child in a Powerful Interaction, open your eyes, your mind, and your heart to her. Let yourself see the interesting and significant things the child is showing you right now. When a child feels you right beside her, interested in what she is doing and open to her agenda rather than your own, a connection happens.

Staying open allows you to see and appreciate a child in a way that you can't when you think you already know all about the child. Children are always growing and changing. No matter how long you've known a child, there is always something new to learn. And, when you convey to children what you are learning about them, they know that you're paying attention and that you care. A connection is formed.

Watch and listen as these teachers use what they're learning in the moment to show interest in and appreciation for that child.

Sixteen-month-old Mai See plays in the doll area. Rachel, her caregiver, sits quietly with a smile on her face, watching to see how Mai See's pretending skills are developing. As Mai See rocks a doll in her arms, Rachel also pretends to hold a baby and makes the same rocking motion. Mai See smiles and then holds her baby out to Rachel.

Nasir, 6 years old, is on the computer writing a story about insects. He has a book open beside the keyboard. Ms. Angela is curious to find out how he's using the book, and she knows that if she's patient and stays in the moment, Nasir will begin the conversation himself. She sits in the chair next to him. After a few moments he says, "I want to put some facts about their habitat in my story. I didn't know everything, so I got this book." Ms. Angela replies, "Nasir, that's a really good idea. Books are an excellent reference material. I'm glad you're finding the information you need."

Different Ways to Learn Something about a Child

Sometimes you learn something about a child when you least expect it. You're observing and interacting, and suddenly there it is! You can use this new piece of information to connect with the child, as Ms. Becky does in this example.

Kayla says, "Look," and pulls up one leg of her purple pants to show Ms. Becky her purple socks. "You sure like purple," says Ms. Becky. "I never knew that. Purple is one of my favorite colors, too. Would you like to read *Harold and the Purple Crayon* together?" "Yes!" says Kayla, and she goes over to the bookshelf to find the little purple book.

At other times, you intentionally create an opportunity to learn something about a child. You might offer a manageable challenge or a new material and observe how the child responds. Notice how Mrs. Franklin connects with Benjamin by offering him a new tool and using what she learns during their interaction to deepen her connection with him.

Mrs. Franklin holds out a wooden spoon to Benjamin, a child who usually stands back and watches, and says, "Would you like to help me make pancakes for snack today?" He smiles shyly and reaches for the spoon. As they mix the flour, sugar, and salt, Benjamin tells her, "Daddy and me make pancakes. But not now. Daddy went away — to Afghanistan." "I didn't know your daddy had already left to do his army work," Mrs. Franklin says. "How about if I take a photo of you making pancakes? Then we can send it to him." Benjamin looks at her, thinks for a moment, and then says, "He can hang it on his wall."

There are still other times when you might not realize you've learned something about a child until you've had some time to reflect on the situation. Perhaps you're looking at a photo you took of a child, reviewing some notes you jotted down, or telling a child's parent a story at the end of the day, and a new realization hits you. Below, Mr. Wilson recalls learning something about 3-year-old Emilena at the end of the day, after all the children had gone home.

"The day had been busier than normal, so I allowed myself to just sit down in the armchair and look back over the photos I took, as a way of reviewing the day. I came to a photo of a child and my assistant working with stacking rings, and in the background I noticed Emilena, standing up and holding on to her walker next to her cot. I couldn't believe my eyes! She must have gotten herself off the cot without help, and that has never happened before. I can't wait to connect with her tomorrow morning, show her this photo, and give her a high-five! And, at the end of the day, I'll let her mom know, too."

Tips to Keep Learning about Children

Stay open to the possibility of what you might learn about the children. The possibilities are endless and amazing. Thinking you know everything about them is like wearing blinders, and it limits what you can see. Here are a few ideas to help you use this strategy to connect with children.

Assess children's progress over time. Observe and record what you see and hear a child doing and saying. Keep track of your observations, as well as children's work, in a portfolio or teacher folder. These objective records will help you continue learning about children as they develop and learn throughout the year. The notes are also helpful when it comes time to share what you know about a child with the child's family or another teacher.

Watch and listen to a child carefully. You can't learn something unless you give children time and space to be themselves. When you join children in what they are doing, be patient so they can learn and solve problems in their own style. For example, you might give an infant the chance to reach for a rattle that rolled away, watch as a toddler works to hang her coat up on the hook, or wait to see what book a preschooler chooses when she goes over to sit in the reading area. You will learn more by watching and listening than by jumping in.

Use what you learn about a child to learn even more. Remember Mrs. Franklin and Benjamin from the earlier example? Mrs. Franklin explains, "It's not enough to just observe and file away new information you learn about a child. I followed up with Benjamin the next day and invited him to talk about the specifics of his father's army job."

Talk with families. Invite family members in to observe their children. Share your new discoveries about the children together.

Use mirror talk to tell children what you are learning about them. *Mirror talk* (an **Extend Learning** strategy described later in this book) lets children know that you see the interesting and significant things they are doing.

You might learn that...	To connect, you might say...
Aden doesn't like loud noises.	"Aden, you came over to hold my hand. I don't think you like those loud noises."
Belicia can peel an orange on her own.	"Wow, Belicia! You're an expert orange peeler."
Sammy knows many songs.	"Sammy, you know many songs. Perhaps you can teach us one that we don't know."
Felipa has been to Mexico.	"Your mom brought in this picture of you with your uncle in Mexico. I didn't know you took a trip there."

How's It Going?

As you keep learning about children, look for clues that this **Connect** strategy is having a positive impact on your relationships with children, your teaching, and your relationships with families.

You may notice children responding to you in new ways. A child may

- Tell you something he's learning about himself: "I never knew I could jump so high!"
- Tell you what she's learned about another child or about you: "I didn't know you like rice and beans, too"
- Connect with you in a new way, such as taking hold of your hand and singing "I like frogs. You like frogs" as you walk together

As you learn more about individual children, you may find that you

- Change your perspective about a child who pushes your buttons

  Kayla's constant motion used to annoy Ms. Becky until she discovered that Kayla likes to sing and she started singing with her. Finding something fun to do together led to Ms. Becky's discovery that Kayla likes purple — and so much more.

- Add something new to your room

  Learning that Benjamin's father had been deployed led Mrs. Franklin to add books such as *I Miss You! A Military Kid's Book About Deployment* (by Beth Andrews) to the bookshelf. She also decided that in future intake interviews with new families, she will ask whether anyone in the family is in the military.

- Begin observing children in different interest areas and focusing your observations on different areas of development. Perhaps you used to spend a lot of time in the housekeeping area observing children's social play and language, but now you're expanding your investigations into the other areas and even outdoors. You're seeing yourself as an explorer — always learning about children.

You may notice stronger relationships with family members as you

● Send a note home to a child's family, sharing a brief story about a Powerful Interaction. In response, you get a phone call or a note describing the family's latest discovery about their child

● Talk with a child about how much you love something — flowers, perhaps. You learn from the child that her parents have a garden. Later that week you get a bunch of daffodils from the family's garden

● Chat with a parent at the end of the day about your interests. The parent volunteers to come and share something with the children that she likes to do, such as cook or play the violin

REALITY

CHECK

Sometimes, a child's unique blend of personality, energy, learning style, and interests can combine to push your buttons. This makes it hard to get to know and appreciate that child as an individual. (The same is sometimes true for a family.) Being professional involves putting extra effort into getting to know your "button-pushers." You may have to work a little harder to pay attention and learn something about them so you can connect.

Remember: *You can use what you learn about a child to connect and strengthen your relationship, then fuel a Powerful Interaction.*

Listen to Children

Listening is more than just hearing. It means deciding to pay attention to find meaning in what someone says — or doesn't say — with his words and/or body language.

Pay attention to children to discover what they are saying with their words or body language, and let them know you have heard them.

How does it feel to listen to someone? Here's what some teachers have to say:

- *I listen best when I'm open to what is going on for the other person.*
- *I try to be quiet and not interrupt.*
- *I find it helps me pay attention if I look at the person's face when she is talking.*

How does it feel when someone listens carefully to you? When someone is open, doesn't interrupt, and pays attention to what you say?

Listen to Connect with Children

Listening to children is one way of telling them

- I care about you
- I am interested in who you are
- I want to know more about what you are doing and thinking

When you truly listen to children, you begin to create a community in which you and children learn from each other about yourselves, each other, and the larger world. As Vygotsky's work highlights (1978), it is through interactions with people that learning and development occur.

Your relationships and connection with children are nurtured as children, knowing their voices are heard, grow to feel more competent and confident. This is an important part of a Powerful Interaction.

There are different ways to listen to children. When a child has the words to communicate her message, you may be able to rely on your ears to catch what she's saying, as Shelley does.

> At the top of the jungle gym, 4-year-old Renata calls, "I climbed to the top! Hooray for me! I'm a good climber." When Shelley, her teacher, responds, "I see you! You climbed all the way to the top! Hooray for you!" she shows she is listening by reflecting back Renata's pleasure in her accomplishment. Shelley then uses the connection she has established with Renata to introduce a new word and concept to this very verbal child. She calls up to Renata, "What do you see from your perspective way up there at the top of the mountain?" ... A Powerful Interaction is well under way.

Children may use means other than words to get their message across. Pay attention to a child's vocal sounds, gestures, facial expressions, and actions, as well as any words he might use, then draw upon what you already know about the child to pull some meaning from what you observe.

> Amanda, 7 months old, is on the changing table, holding her fresh diaper in front of her face. She peeks around it and catches Ms. Lynette's eye. Ms. Lynette connects with Amanda by showing her she is "listening" to what Amanda is "telling" her. "I see you," she says. "I think you are telling me

you want to play peekaboo. That's been your favorite game lately, hasn't it?" As she continues changing Amanda, Ms. Lynette plays along with the peekaboo game, creating a Powerful Interaction in which she can extend Amanda's learning by helping her explore the concept that *out of sight* is not the same as *gone forever*.

Two-year-old Joey falls down on the sidewalk. "I'm okay," he says as Mrs. Rogers helps him up, though his lower lip quivers and tears gather in his eyes. Knowing that Joey often tries to hold back his feelings, Mrs. Rogers decides to connect with him and begin a Powerful Interaction about feelings by giving Joey words for what she knows he is not saying. "Sometimes falling down can really hurt," she says. "Shall we look at your leg and see if you need a bandage? Maybe your teddy bear wants one, too." Sniffling, Joey nods and reaches for his teacher's hand.

Nora, age 5, bounces in her seat during a conversation at snack time. Wendy, her teacher, kneels down and places her hand gently on Nora's shoulder. Knowing that Nora understands much more than she can say in English, Wendy connects with the child: "Nora, I think you have something to say but might not have all the English words you need to say it yet. Do you want to say something about this juicy pineapple we are eating?" Nora says, "Po. I mean yes. *Po* is Albanian. *Yes* is English." Wendy says, "That's right. You taught me an Albanian word. *Po* means *yes*. And here's a new word for you: *pineapple*." Nora, with a big grin, says, "I like pineapple."

Tips for Listening to Children

The way you listen to a child can reassure him that he is valued, or it can discourage the child from talking further to you. As you seek to make a connection with children by watching and listening to what they have to tell you, keep in mind some listening dos and don'ts.

Put yourself at the child's level. Sit or kneel. Look into the child's eyes. *Don't* — Listen while you are busy with something else, or turn away while a child is talking.

Give a child time to gather his or her thoughts. *Don't* — Fill the child's silence with your own words.

Convey "I hear you" as the child talks by nodding; raising your eyebrows; tilting your head; opening your eyes wide; saying "Mmmm," "Uh-huh," or "I understand" and "I see what you mean" (if you truly do). *Don't* — Interrupt or finish a child's sentence.

Acknowledge the child's feelings. "You look and sound like you are angry." *Don't* — Assign feelings to a child: "That made you angry."

Teach children to wait while you listen to another child, so they don't interrupt. *Don't* — Be distracted by or turn your attention to another child. Encourage waiting by:

● Thanking children for their patience: "Thank you for waiting so I could listen to Eugene the way I listened to you."

● Suggesting that they help each other: "Peter, I can't tie your shoes right now, but Stevie knows how. Perhaps you could ask him to help you."

How's It Going?

What do you see happening as you take the time to really listen to children? Look for these clues that your efforts are having a positive impact on children, families, your program, and yourself.

As children sense your genuine interest in them, they may

● Tell you more stories about what they do and feel

● Call you over more often to tell you about their work

● Imitate you — your facial expression and words — as they listen to their dolls, stuffed animals, and each other during dramatic play

Family members may

● Say they appreciate how you always seem to have time to listen to their children

● Listen more purposefully to children — their own and others — after seeing you do it and talking with you about the importance of listening to children

As you make stronger connections with children and their families through listening, you may be surprised, amazed, or touched by the new things you learn. You may find it exciting to discover ways to further children's learning based on your new knowledge.

In your program, people of all ages may interrupt each other less often. Children may make more of an effort to wait patiently as you finish listening to another child, knowing they will have a chance to connect with you later. Family members and colleagues, too, may wait, secure in knowing that you will listen to them, as well.

Your space may feel a tiny bit quieter and calmer as teachers, children, and family members spend more time listening to and connecting with one another.

Remember: *When you really listen to children, you deepen your relationship with them and open the door to learning. Gradually, you'll find that as you practice Step One: Be Present and quiet the static in your mind, you can listen more attentively.*

Personalize
Your Interactions

Doesn't it feel great when you go into a store and the cashier calls you by name? She remembers you. You are not just another customer. There is a connection between you, and it feels good. You're likely to go back, not only to buy more milk or eggs but also to reconnect and build on your relationship.

Adjust what you do and say to connect with a child and to respond to what the child needs in that moment.

Do you have favorite stores or restaurants you return to because you have a personal connection with someone there? How has your relationship grown with time and repeated interactions?

Relate to Each Child as an Individual

Using what you know about a child, you can tailor what you say and do to fit her personality, needs, strengths, and interests.

Your willingness to personalize your interaction lets the child know that you are paying attention to her, right now, in the moment. What you're doing and saying is for and about her. You're telling her that she matters. When you respond to what a child needs in the moment, you create a connection. This connection builds on your relationship, allowing the child to settle in and be more receptive to the possibilities for learning in a Powerful Interaction.

Meet Mayra and Claire. They are both 2½ years old and love puzzles.

When Mayra puts a puzzle together, she picks up pieces quickly, tries each one in a spot, and if it doesn't fit, she puts it back on the table and picks up the next piece. She chatters as she works.

When Claire works on puzzles, she moves slowly and quietly. She picks up each piece, looks at it, looks at the puzzle frame, and then picks out a spot to try. If it doesn't fit, she looks again and tries the piece in another spot.

Now meet the girls' teacher, Stacey. She shares these examples of how she personalizes her interactions to reflect each child's personality and approach to working on a puzzle.

"As I walk toward her, Mayra looks up from her puzzle, smiles, and says, 'Come here. Look!' 'Hi, Mayra,' I say as I sit down next to her. I tell her what I see. 'Mayra, you're trying lots of different pieces.' 'Yep,' she says, as she puts one down and picks up another. I ask a question to focus her thinking and actions: 'What do you think would happen if you turned that piece around and tried it again?'

"With Claire, I move in more slowly and quietly. I sit beside her and watch. She keeps her attention on the puzzle, but I feel her leg brush mine. Only when she is stuck does she look at me. I tell her what I see in a calm and quiet voice: 'Claire, you really study each piece carefully.' I ask her about her observations: 'What do you notice about that piece? What do you notice about that empty space?'"

How did Stacey personalize her interactions?

- She observed the children to learn about each one's unique characteristics and approach to solving a puzzle.

- She adjusted her tempo and volume to fit each child's personality.

- She told each child exactly what she saw her doing (the strategy of *mirror talk* described in **Extend Learning** later in this book).

- She used what she knew about each child and what she learned from observing in the current situations to ask different questions that support different problem-solving strategies.

Tips for Personalizing Your Interactions with Children

As you considered Step One: Be Present, you thought about how to adjust inside yourself to be present for a child.

Now, like Stacey did, it's time to adjust what you say and do to find the just-right fit and to connect with that child. To connect by personalizing your interaction, ask yourself, "What does this child need from me in this moment?"

Different tips work for different children. Here are some strategies to try:

Use the child's name.

Learn and use words from the child's home language.

Slow down or speed up your interaction dance to be in step with the child.

Adjust the volume and tone of your voice to match the child's personality and mood.

Make adjustments to support a child who may have special needs. For example, make sure a child who is deaf can see your face and lips when you are talking.

Choose words that fit with the child's level of language development.

Change the expression on your face to fit the situation and the child's emotions.

Use hand gestures that will help the child understand your words.

How's It Going?

As you practice personalizing your interactions, look for clues that this strategy is affecting your relationships with children and families. Here are some signs you may notice in your program.

Children will let you know when you are responding to them as individuals. They may

- Grow more confident and competent
- Develop specials ways of connecting with you — waving, smiling, winking — that they don't do with anyone else
- Show you they feel close to you, as when Claire brushed her leg against Stacey's
- Focus longer or more deeply on an activity when you are present

You may notice that you

- Slip into automatic "teacher talk" less often, because you are tailoring how you speak to the needs of individual children
- Offer children new and different learning opportunities that reflect their specific interests and challenge them

As you make an effort to connect with family members as individuals, they may share more about themselves. Perhaps they volunteer to teach children a song they used to sing as a child, or cook a food from their childhood for snack time.

Your setting may start to include more photos, music, and objects that reflect families' cultures and traditions.

Remember: *When you connect with a child by modifying your words and actions to fit her personality, interests, strengths, and needs, you enrich your relationship and make it more possible for her to take advantage of the learning opportunities in a Powerful Interaction.*

Show Respect

Respectful interactions come in all shapes and sizes. Think about how you might feel in these situations:

- Someone opens a door for you because your arms are full of grocery bags.

- A driver stops to let you cross the street safely.

- A neighbor comes by with a vase of flowers because he knows you haven't been feeling well.

- You and your brother don't see eye-to-eye about politics, but you have good discussions in which you both listen to each other.

Now think about children and how respectful interactions affect them.

> *Use words and actions that are kind, courteous, considerate, and attentive and that show children you value them.*

Respectful Interactions with Children

Showing respect is a key way to connect with a child and strengthen a positive relationship. When you show a child respect, the child knows you care about and value him. Your respect reminds the child of the trust and caring between you, and it makes him feel more confident and competent to explore and learn in a Powerful Interaction.

Read Aaron's story, alone or out loud with your teaching partner. Try to put yourself in Aaron's shoes. How does his teacher, Valerie, connect with him by showing him respect?

The Day Aaron Forgot His Lunch Box

"One day Mom and I left my lunch box at home. Mom would have been late for work if we went back for it, so I had to go to preschool without it. I was really worried. What would I eat for snack and lunch? I was crying really hard.

"My teacher, Miss Valerie, met me at the door like she always does. At first she was smiling, but stopped when she noticed my tears. She knelt down and said, 'Oh, dear, Aaron! You're crying. You look upset about something. How can I help you feel better?' I tried to tell her, but all I could say was 'lunch box.' But she figured it out, 'You forgot your lunch box? Are you worried what you'll eat all day?' In between sobs, I nodded.

"Other kids had arrived and everyone was staring at me. Valerie took me by the hand, my mother following behind us. In the kitchen area, Valerie showed me cans of soup, jars of peanut butter and jelly, some bread, and a bag of apples. She said, 'Aaron, I remember that you often bring a peanut butter and jelly sandwich for lunch. And last week when we made soup, you said you like soup. At outside time, would you like to stay inside for a few minutes so Mr. Wally can help you make your lunch?'

"By this time, I wasn't crying so much, so I said yes and asked if I could have an apple for snack. Valerie let me pick out the one I wanted, which I washed and put in my cubby. After that, the day got better."

Did you notice how Valerie connected with Aaron when she

- Used Aaron's name as she talked with him
- Changed her facial expression to match Aaron's emotions
- Knelt on the floor to be at his eye level
- Acknowledged his tears and said, "Oh, dear, Aaron! You're crying."
- Asked Aaron how she could help him
- Listened to Aaron's words and made sense of them
- Respected his privacy by taking his hand and leading him away from the group
- Used her observations of Aaron's preferences to offer lunch choices
- Included Aaron in finding a solution to the problem

Tips for Showing Respect

Here are some simple ways you can show children you respect them, giving a boost to their confidence and feelings of competence:

Use a warm, calm, and natural tone of voice.

Talk *with* children, rather than at them or about them.

Listen attentively when children talk to you.

Be polite; avoid teasing, put-downs, or sarcasm.

Talk to children in private when guiding their behavior; remind them of reasons for rules, and discuss what they can do differently.

Ask children's permission before you touch them: "Oh, you got a haircut yesterday. Can I touch your head to see what it feels like?"

Give children — and yourself — a fresh start each day. Let go of frustrations from yesterday and be open to the possibilities today brings.

REMIND YOURSELF

On a sticky note, write one suggestion for showing respect each week. Put the note in a place where you can see it. Try to make it a habit to follow your suggestion!

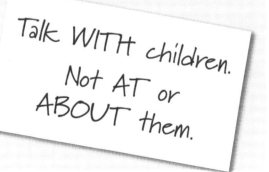

Talk WITH children. Not AT or ABOUT them.

REALITY

CHECK

There will always be children you like more than others. You don't have to like every child, but being professional means that you must show every child respect.

How's It Going?

As you incorporate respectful interactions into your day-to-day practice, you're likely to notice positive effects on children, family members, and your environment. Look for these clues that your efforts are paying off.

Children will show that they feel respected by you by respecting each other. You may see children

- Helping each other
- Spending more time in pairs or trios than alone
- Sharing materials more easily
- Asking for turns
- Listening to each other's stories
- Showing more affection for each other
- Saying please and thank you
- Apologizing for a mistake without being reminded

Family members may be more willing to share their parenting questions and challenges with you when they feel that by showing respect, you're connecting with their children, and thus with them.

You may be feeling more comfortable working with and connecting with more diverse children and families — for example, a family from a cultural and ethnic group you do not yet know much about, or a child or family member who has a physical or an emotional disability.

Your space may reflect your respect for and connection with children. For example, you declutter the walls and display children's art so that it can be seen and appreciated. Or, your bookshelf includes books you have written with the children about their everyday experiences, such as *Yvanna Steps in a Puddle* or *Francisco Has a New Cat*.

Remember: *Connecting with children by showing respect makes your positive relationships with children stronger, giving them the foundation of trust and security they need to be confident, capable learners.*

Guide Children's Behavior

Think of a situation in which you weren't sure how you were expected to behave. Perhaps you felt this way when you

- Started working in a new program
- Went back to school after having been away for several years
- Joined friends from a different culture at a ceremonial occasion
- Visited a new country, or a community very different from your own

Help children behave in positive ways by setting clear limits, modeling cooperative behavior, and dealing respectfully with challenging behaviors.

Was there someone who guided you so that you could feel more comfortable, confident, and competent? What did that person do and say to guide you? Afterward, how did you feel about the person who helped you?

Connect with Children by Guiding Behavior in Positive Ways

Guiding children's behavior is something done throughout the day, not just when a child acts in a way that is unsafe or unacceptable. You *guide* behavior by establishing predictable routines, setting clear rules with children, and modeling kindness and respect. You are also attentive and aware of what is going on. Together, these actions help children feel noticed, confident, and secure. Children experience your attention and guidance as a caring embrace holding everything together. They know you're on their team.

Sometimes a child's behavior calls for more specific and direct attention from you. In these moments, reacting with negative emotion — instead of being calm and deliberate — can undermine the positive relationship you're working to build with that child.

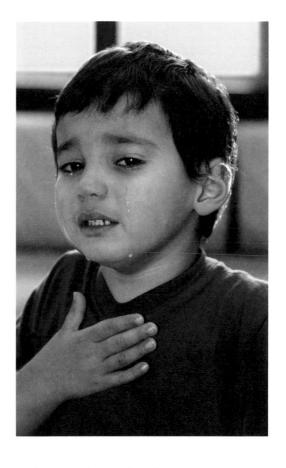

These challenging situations can be turned in a positive direction when you remember that you want the child to feel you are on her team. When you demonstrate this by connecting with the child to deepen your relationship, you make it possible for her to learn new, more positive behaviors.

You open the door to a Powerful Interaction when you

- **Treat the child the way you want him to treat you and others** — The children you care for and teach look up to you and want to be like you. When you model positive, cooperative behavior, they will be more likely to interact with each other in positive ways.

Ms. Cate makes every effort to treat Robert, a large, active, and at times aggressive first-grader, with respect. It pays off the day she watches in delight as Robert walks over to a group of children on the playground and, instead of pushing his way in and trying to grab the ball, asks, "Can I play?" Later she says to him, "Way to go, Robert. I see you asked to join the game." She begins a Powerful Interaction to affirm his new behaviors for entering a game.

● **Help a child feel secure by setting clear, realistic limits for behavior** — When you set limits, you build trust between you and children by giving them the security that comes with knowing what to expect and what is expected of them. Limits also help you teach children about what is safe, acceptable behavior. Here are two examples from Mrs. Greene's family child care home:

At lunchtime, Amanda reaches for a butter knife and proudly spreads some hummus on a cracker. Still holding the knife, she gets up and heads for the dress-up corner. "Amanda," says Mrs. Greene. "Remember our rule: *Sit at the table when you're using a knife.* Would you like to come sit down and eat your cracker? Or would you like to give me your knife, wash your hands, and go play?" Amanda looks at Mrs. Greene, then at the knife in her hand. She comes back to the table. "Now you can enjoy that crunchy cracker," says Mrs. Greene with a smile. Amanda smiles back through the crumbs.

At naptime, Mrs. Greene hums softly while rocking Kylie, the baby in her mixed-age group. Kylie reaches up and tugs hard on Mrs. Greene's hair. Gently pulling Kylie's hand away, Mrs. Greene says softly, "That hurts. Let's be gentle with each other." Mrs. Greene rubs her hand gently on Kylie's head.

● **Manage your emotions so that you can help children manage theirs** — Extreme behaviors, such as a temper tantrum, biting, or hitting, are the result of children's strong emotions. You are likely to have a strong emotional reaction to these behaviors, as well. In these situations, children need you on their team more than ever. When you draw on your positive relationship and the feeling of connection that has developed between you over time, you can respond in a way that benefits the child, strengthens your relationship, and enables the child to learn from the situation. Watch as Mr. Vargas uses a Powerful Interaction to prevent biting and to connect with Lee:

Mr. Vargas has been keeping a close eye on 3-year-old Lee since Lee bit another child earlier this morning. He notices Lee heading for the cardboard box house, where two other children are playing. "That could be trouble," he thinks. Mr. Vargas scans the room. The other children are busy playing. Taking a calming breath, he nods at his teaching partner to let her know he's going to focus on Lee. Then he heads toward the house. Mr. Vargas does a quick Me Check: "I know I'm still upset about Lee biting this morning. I bet he's upset, too. I need to let go of my irritation with him and stay really calm so that I don't add any more tension to our interaction."

As Mr. Vargas approaches, Lee is pushing his way into the house. As the other children protest, Lee pushes on the door harder. As Lee leans toward Karey's arm and opens his mouth, Mr. Vargas steps in. Gently but firmly grasping Lee's shoulders, Mr. Vargas says quietly, "Lee, I'm not going to let you bite Karey. I'll help you join in the play." Lee looks up at him. After a few seconds he leans in against Mr. Vargas and his face relaxes a little bit. They connect.

Sometimes a child's biting or other behavior can be so extreme that your focus must be stopping the behavior and protecting everyone's safety. Even in these situations, children deserve and need you to be present and respectful, rather than angry. Some additional guidance from a mental health professional may be needed to help you support the child.

REALITY **CHECK** *Sometimes your feelings may get in the way of making the best decisions about what to say and do in a Powerful Interaction. This happens. When it does, be sure to take some steps to reconnect with the child in a positive way so that you can continue to strengthen your relationship.*

Tips for Guiding Children's Behavior

Remember that you guide children's behavior each day as you interact with them. Some ways you can do this include the following:

Be realistic about what you can expect from individual children. Take into account a child's age and what is happening in that child's life as you consider what kind of guidance he needs. For example,

> It makes sense that Roger, whose mother is in the hospital, is scared, angry, and worried. He needs extra help from you to deal with his feelings of anger, frustration, fear, and worry and to avoid fighting with other children.

Scan your room regularly to anticipate problems. Who needs your guidance in a Powerful Interaction? Are there any potential behavior situations brewing?

> Perhaps you notice that Alicia is playing with blocks and her tower keeps falling over. What might happen next? You might think, "Her mom told me she didn't sleep much last night. I can see her getting frustrated. How can I interact to prevent a problem from starting? I'm going to go over and sit down next to her."

Coordinate with your teaching partner. Recall that Mr. Vargas signaled his co-teacher with a nod as he went to help Lee. Learn to cue each other about where and when to interact to prevent conflict and tension.

Partner with families. Let families know how important it is for you to know about issues that arise at home day by day. The news they share in the morning about a child's sleeping, eating, toileting, mood, and changes in routine at home helps you anticipate and guide children's behavior at school in positive ways. For example,

> When you know Aaron didn't get much sleep, you might offer him an early nap or be sure he has space in a stroller when you walk to the park, so his tiredness doesn't cause a tantrum.

Take a long-term view. Remember that learning how to behave and get along with others takes time and experience. Some of us are still learning.

Here are some tips for dealing with a challenging behavior:

Put aside your feelings. Too often, challenging behavior pits you and the child against each other. Remember that you are on the same team.

Make it clear that the problem is the child's behavior, not the child. It's the biting, hitting, or pushing that you want to stop — or better yet, prevent. Find ways to reassure children that you have not stopped liking *them*.

Use a tone of voice that is firm and serious, but calm rather than angry when addressing a child's behavior. Anger is scary, and when children feel scared they cannot learn anything.

Keep and use your sense of humor. When appropriate for the child and the situation, a silly face, dance, rhyme, or joke can release tension like magic.

How's It Going?

Are you connecting with children and building a foundation for learning as you encourage positive behavior in Powerful Interactions? Here are some clues that the answer is yes:

Children may

- Be more relaxed and at ease
- Use some of the same language you use to guide behavior as they work and play with their peers: "Hitting isn't safe" … "Don't forget to use your words" … "We might not have enough space here for all of us to work together"
- Use some of the same language to remind themselves: For example, you might notice Jorge start to run across the room, then slow down as he says to himself, "We walk inside"

You may

- Use a calmer voice as you guide challenging behaviors
- Anticipate more situations, and notice that fewer challenging behaviors are occurring
- Have more positive relationships with children who were pushing your buttons because of their challenging behaviors

Family members may

- Begin talking more about encouraging positive behavior than about making children behave
- Ask you for advice about how to encourage such behavior, and share stories of how they encourage it at home

You may also notice that the overall climate of your program is calmer as children learn positive behaviors.

Remember: *Guiding children's behavior is a way to connect and strengthen your relationships with them, making it possible to transform a potential behavior problem into a learning opportunity.*

Keep Trust Growing

Think of someone you trust.

How do you feel when you're together? What is it about this person that allows you to trust?

Here's what some other teachers have to say about a person they trust:

Through many interactions over time, consistently give children your attention and respond to their signals so that they feel safe and secure.

- *My grandfather always had time to listen.*
- *I think about my sister. She's always there for me. I can count on her.*
- *I really trust my best friend because she knows what I need.*
- *When I think about a teacher that I really trusted, my second grade teacher comes to mind. All these years later I can remember raising my hand and knowing that she would accept and appreciate my ideas.*

Being Trustworthy with Children

Trust is the foundation of positive relationships and learning. When children trust you, they feel safe letting you know how they feel and what matters to them. There is a connection between you that allows children to explore and take risks as they learn about the world.

Here you will see how Janice, a teacher at a child care center, uses the daily routine of morning arrival to further her relationship of trust with Sophia.

This morning traffic was heavier than usual, and Janice got to the center a little late. She feels stressed.

"Yesterday Miss Janice remembered that my favorite color is red. I wonder if she'll notice my new red sneakers?"

Then 3-year-old Sophia arrives. Standing in the doorway with a shy grin on her face, Sophia glances down at her new red sneakers, then over at Janice.

Noticing the child's expression, Janice puts down what she's doing and joins Sophia at the door. She kneels down: "Sophia, you have new red sneakers! They are red like your daddy's jacket and your favorite color. Your feet have been growing so fast. Your old sneakers got too small for you."

"That little grin is Sophia's quiet way of inviting me to interact. Mixing this paint will wait. I want to connect and show her she can trust me to pay attention and care about her."

Sophia lifts one tiny foot to give Janice a closer look at her sneaker. Janice smiles, and the memory of the traffic and her stress fade away. ... Her day with the children begins.

A child learns to trust adults through their actions and words. Janice noticed and responded to Sophia's signal that she wanted Janice's attention. Through many small interactions like this one, Sophia learns that she can trust Janice. Their relationship is strengthened, and Janice uses this opportunity to begin a Powerful Interaction about *size* and the color *red*.

Like Janice, you can connect with children by earning their trust, little by little, over time. And, like Sophia, children will begin to see that they can count on you for enjoyable moments of connection — moments that help them feel safe, seen, and understood.

Tips for Keeping Trust Growing

Watch children carefully, and tell them what you see and hear. This lets them know you're paying attention. Janice did this when she noticed Sophia's grin and went over to admire her sneakers.

Listen and respond so children know you care about them. Sophia "spoke" to Janice without saying a word. Janice "listened" and responded to Sophia's facial expression and body language. Other times, a child may be more vocal with a request for your attention.

> When Sara calls, "Come see my block building!" you might say, "I can't wait to see it! I'll be right over after I finish playing this game with Justin."

Talk with children about their families so that a child feels connected to her family members when they are apart.

REALITY CHECK *Many times you won't be able to go to a child right away. Telling the child when you're coming will let her know you care and will help her learn how to wait.*

> Later that morning, as Janice takes Sophia and a few other children on a color walk, she says, "This apple reminds me of Sophia's red sneakers and her daddy's red jacket."

Keep the promises you make so children can depend on you.

> Say to 2-year-old Jack, "I promised you that we would read *Goodnight Moon*. So let's read it now!"

Let children know what to expect so that they feel safe and secure.

> Lisa, a family child care provider, says to the children, "Tomorrow Rashani's mother is bringing a special snack, but she can't come at our regular snack time, so we'll go outside before snack instead of after snack. That will feel different, won't it?"

Acknowledge and accept children's emotions so they can learn that it is safe to share their feelings. Let an upset child know you are there to help by giving her a hug, holding her on your lap, or sitting close by and speaking softly.

How's It Going?

Look for clues that you are connecting with children and that trust is growing.

A child may

- Share feelings with you
- Tell you what matters to him
- Explore new objects and materials
- Take risks to try new activities
- Come to you for comfort
- Laugh with you
- Ask you for help
- Imitate your actions and words

Family members may share more, too, as they sense their children's comfort with you.

You may feel energized by your growing connectedness with children, and you may learn new things about them.

Your program setting may feel more relaxed for children, family members, and you.

I had one very quiet child. She cried often and would rarely speak. Since I started doing Powerful Interactions with her, she's really opened up. Now she gives me a hug and starts conversations. She initiates play with me. She responds to my questions and shows excitement at getting my focused attention. She's more relaxed, and it seems she has an easier time being herself. And, boy, do I see how much she really knows and how much she can really do. I don't think I would have noticed so much had I not used Powerful Interactions.

— Darice (a preschool teacher)

Remember: *As trust develops between you and the children in your setting, your relationships grow stronger. As they work, play, and learn, children will be more likely to deeply engage with you and one another.*

STEP THREE: EXTEND LEARNING

*As you nurture your relationship,
stretch the child's knowledge
and understanding*

STEP ONE: STEP TWO:
BE PRESENT   CONNECT

STEP THREE:
EXTEND LEARNING

As you read this chapter, pause to reflect on what you're learning. How could you use its ideas and strategies in your setting?

STEP THREE:
EXTEND LEARNING

Here you are together — for a minute or maybe five. You've made a connection, and as you sustain that connection, deepening your relationship with the child, you can make the interaction into a Powerful Interaction by simultaneously extending the child's learning just a bit. When children have a strong, positive relationship with you, they feel safe, competent, and able to move out into the world, or "take distance" to explore, experiment, and learn (Sigel 1993). The combination of intentionally building your relationship and extending a child's learning is the essence of a Powerful Interaction.

In Step Three of a Powerful Interaction, you not only model for the child how to learn, you also stretch the child's thinking and knowledge — all in a way that is just right for that child. No matter what you teach, how you interact as you do it influences how well children learn it. Children who have positive relationships with their teachers also are more engaged in learning. When they feel the comfort and security that comes from a trusting relationship, children are more willing to explore, ask questions, solve problems, try new challenges, and express their thinking (O'Connor & McCartney 2007).

You met the teachers in the following examples in the chapter Step Two: Connect. Now, let's look at how they use their relationships with the children as the foundation for extending each child's learning:

> As Ms. Zora joins 2-year-old Dennis at the sandbox, she initiates a connection with him by giving him a warm smile. She says, "Hi, Dennis! I've been watching you digging this great big hole. Your muscles are getting such a workout!" Dennis looks up at Ms. Zora with a huge grin on his face. Opening his eyes wide, he says to her, "Big hole!"... Ms. Zora models curiosity and encourages him to make a prediction about size: "I wonder what could fit in that hole. What do you think might fit in that hole, Dennis?" She waits for Dennis to respond. After a moment, she asks, "Should we try this ball? Will it fit or will it be too big? What do you think, Dennis?" Dennis takes the ball from Ms. Zora and puts it in the hole. It fits and he laughs!

Three-year-old Celia has dumped a basket of smooth stones on the rug and is putting them back in one by one, saying a number in random order each time. Mr. Yosef settles in next to her on the floor and, leaning in toward her just a little bit, comments: "I heard all these numbers and wondered who was practicing their counting. It's Celia!" She says, "Wanna watch me?" ... She counts to 5, randomly pointing to the stones. To extend her learning Mr. Yosef decides to help her move from random counting to one-to-one object counting. "Shall we count them together?" Celia nods her head. Mr. Yosef models how to count objects. He says, "Let's get our fingers ready to point. We'll point to each one as we say the number. Ready?" Celia sticks out her finger and together they point and count.

Slowly and methodically, 4-year-old Khalid looks through every book on the bookshelf. Mr. Hall watches him and decides to initiate a Powerful Interaction. He silently kneels beside him and joins in his search for a good book. After a few seconds, Khalid takes one of the books off the shelf, holds it in his lap, and begins turning the pages slowly. Sitting quietly beside Khalid, Mr. Hall watches to see the child's body settle and senses that he is getting comfortable with the teacher's presence before beginning to talk about the book. ... To extend his learning, Mr. Hall says, "I'm curious about the book you're looking at, Khalid. The pictures of the shoes look very interesting. Can we look at it together?" Khalid turns to look at him, slides the book over so that it is between them, points to a pair of cowboy boots, and says, "These are my favorite." A back-and-forth conversation about what Khalid is reading and noticing in the book begins. Mr. Hall makes sure to bring out key concepts about print and interesting vocabulary during their conversation.

What Does It Mean to "Extend Learning"?

A Powerful Interaction is a teachable moment with a child — a chance for skillful and deliberate teaching. During a Powerful Interaction, you have a window into the child's experience and thinking, because in this moment, your attention is focused on the child — her actions and/or language.

In this rich teaching moment, you stay present, so that you can intentionally make sensitive and responsive decisions about the individual child's learning needs. Just as you need to be alert to how the child reacts each time you invite a connection, the teaching strategy you choose in Step Three may need to shift as children learn and develop, each in his or her own unique way.

"The greatest opportunity for learning lies in moments of teacher-child interaction, when the teacher crafts learning experiences that stretch children just beyond their current skill level."

— Munro 2008, 47

Three questions will help you make effective decisions about how to extend that child's learning. We examine each question separately so you can understand and think about each one carefully.

1. **What's the right content to teach in this moment?** Being present and focused on the child (Step One: Be Present) and observing what is interesting and significant about what the child is doing (Step Two: Connect) help you know what the child needs from you in order to learn in this moment. Is the child talking? If so, you might decide to introduce a new vocabulary word. Perhaps the child is working on cause-and-effect thinking. If so, you might ask, "Why do you think that happened?" Maybe the child is counting or measuring, and you could focus the interaction on math content. Or the child might be trying to sound out a word, and you could decide to help with the sound a certain letter makes.

Deidre, age 4, uses red playdough and cookie cutters to make a series of shapes. She lines them up in a row from left to right. Rhonda, her teacher, watches and recognizes that this is a good moment to extend Deidre's understanding of geometry (because of the shapes) and spatial thinking (because of how she's carefully placing them in a straight row on the table).

2. **What's the next step in this child's learning?** Once you decide on the content area to focus on, you can think about the next small learning step the child is ready to take: What does she already know? What can she already do? By drawing on your knowledge of the child, as well as on your knowledge of the typical sequence of learning steps in that content area, you can decide how to extend the child's learning just a bit in that moment.

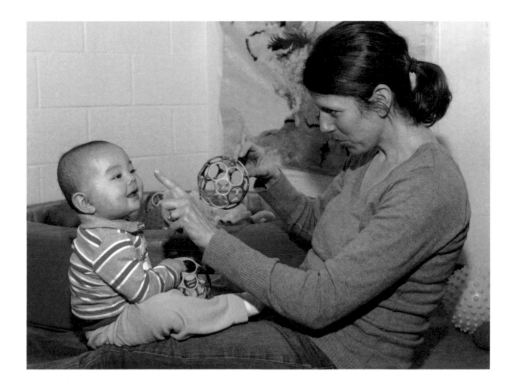

Your goal is to keep the child engaged and learning — but at the same time, feeling safe and secure. If you push her learning too hard or too far, you jeopardize the trusting and secure relationship you have built with the child by making her feel overwhelmed. You want to keep the child interested and curious. You want the child to be successful and motivated to go further the next time.

Using the strategy of mirror talk, Rhonda says, "Wow. I notice you've carefully placed the playdough shapes in a straight line from left to right." In this way, Rhonda lets Deidre know that she sees her and validates the effort she's made. Rhonda also calls the child's attention to organization and direction, while giving her language to describe what she's done.

3. **How do I make learning meaningful for this child?** Learning is meaningful to children when it relates to their prior experiences or to their interests. You can make learning meaningful by considering what you already know about the child — her knowledge, skills, interests, and life experiences — and paying attention to what's engaging her at the moment. A little patient observing keeps you from disturbing the child's focus or taking her in a direction unrelated to where she is at that moment.

Knowing that Deidre often thinks systematically, Rhonda decides to extend her learning a little more by inviting her to use language to describe her plan. Rhonda says, "I'm curious, Deidre. How did you decide to organize your shapes this way?"

Examples of Extending Learning

Now let's look at a few examples of how teachers make decisions about extending learning in a Powerful Interaction. As you read each one, consider how the teacher's decision resulted in a Powerful Interaction.

Ms. Ramsey and Sherese

Five-month-old Sherese is on the floor, lying on her belly. She stretches her hands out toward the string of a pull-toy turtle, which is just out of reach. Ms. Ramsey watches and thinks before she walks over and gets down on the floor beside Sherese.

"Oh, my, Sherese. Look at you. You're stretching for the turtle's string." Sherese looks at Ms. Ramsey, reaches toward the string again, and makes a little grunting sound. Ms. Ramsey responds, "I wonder what you'll do when you get it. Shall I give you a little push so you can reach it?" She gently slides Sherese's body closer to the string. Sherese grabs it, pulls the turtle close to her, grasps the toy with both of her hands, and giggles with delight. "Look at that! You pulled the string and now you've got the turtle in your hands!"

Ms. Ramsey could have picked the toy up and put it closer to Sherese. But if she had, Sherese would have missed out on the opportunity to achieve her goal and feel competent. Instead, Ms. Ramsey created a Powerful Interaction: She watched what Sherese was doing, thought about the situation, and connected with Sherese. Then she decided to extend Sherese's learning by helping Sherese think about cause and effect. To do this, Ms. Ramsey gave her a little nudge toward the interesting pull toy, then celebrated her success.

Mr. Banks and Tommy

Mr. Banks notices Tommy, 30 months, standing at a low table and lining up several rubber people in a straight row. He looks on for a few minutes to give himself time to think about Tommy and plan a Powerful Interaction. He approaches Tommy, kneels on the floor next to him, and says, "Tommy, this looks like fun. Can I play, too?" Tommy smiles and hands Mr. Banks one of the rubber people.

As Mr. Banks observes, Tommy begins moving the people one by one into a dollhouse. Mr. Banks decides to extend Tommy's learning by focusing on number concepts. "Hey, Tommy, I see you're putting each person in the house. You've put two people in there already and I see that number three is on its way." Tommy smiles at Mr. Banks and says, "Three." As Tommy picks up the next person, he says, "Four." As he picks up the next person, he gives Mr. Banks a questioning look. Mr. Banks responds. "Now there are four people in the house — 1, 2, 3, 4 — and here comes number…?" After a pause, Tommy shouts, "Five!"

Mr. Banks made this a Powerful Interaction by first observing to see what Tommy was doing. Then, to make a connection, he asked Tommy if he could join in the play. Mr. Banks went slowly in order to maintain the positive connection and then extended what Tommy was already doing by creating a playful counting game. This would not have been a Powerful Interaction if Mr. Banks had come up to Tommy and simply asked, "How many people are in the house?"

Ms. Isabel, Deval, and Jacquie

Four-year-old Deval is at the art table. He's cutting out pictures from a magazine and gluing them onto a piece of construction paper to make a collage. Another 4-year-old, Jacquie, is sitting beside him, and they're taking turns telling each other about the pictures in their collages. Deval says, "I have a car." Jacquie says, "I have a skyscraper." Ms. Isabel stands nearby, taking in their back-and-forth game. After a few minutes, she decides to join them.

"I've been listening to you two playing a wonderful game about the pictures in your collages. Can I play along?" The two children agree and Ms. Isabel takes a turn: "I see that both of you have different animals in your collages." Both children scan their collages and Deval speaks up: "Yeah, I have a pony and a giraffe and a bird." Jacquie chimes in: "I've got a panda and a horsie and a butterfly."

Ms. Isabel sees an opportunity to extend their phonological awareness a little bit: "Hey, I heard something similar about your animals! Deval has a pony and Jacquie has a panda. Listen carefully as I say each word. *Pony … panda*. What sound do you hear at the beginning of each word?" Both children make exaggerated /p/ sounds with their lips and say, "P!" The next time it's her turn, Ms. Isabel helps them hear the matching initial sounds of *bird* and *butterfly*. After she leaves, Deval and Jacquie continue the game and find a few other pictures that begin with matching initial sounds.

Ms. Isabel could have rushed in and quizzed each child about the initial sounds of pictures on their collages. This would have likely interrupted their self-initiated game. Instead, she took some time to notice what the two children were doing and came up with a way to extend the game they were already playing and also focus their attention on initial sounds. She succeeded in having a Powerful Interaction with two children at one time.

Mr. Jim, Leah, and Monette

Mr. Jim, a first grade teacher, uses geoboards to teach his students about the perimeter of different shapes. Children are working in pairs to solve a challenge he has given — to create a square and a nonsquare rectangle that have perimeters of the same size using geobands (rubber bands). He watches

Leah, who was born without sight, work on the challenge with Monette. Leah says to Monette, "I made the square and it has a perimeter of 8. What's the perimeter of your rectangle?" Monette says, "I haven't finished it yet."

At this point, Mr. Jim decides to connect with the two girls: "Leah and Monette, you two have really been concentrating on the challenge. Can I sit with you and watch for a minute?" In unison, both girls say, "Sure!" Monette finishes her rectangle and says, "There, my rectangle is done." Leah asks, "What's the perimeter?" Monette says, "I don't know." Mr. Jim sees an opening to extend their learning: "Leah, can you show Monette how to figure out the perimeter of her rectangle?" Leah says, "Show me where your shape is, Monette." Monette takes Leah's hand and puts it on her rectangle. Leah says, "Now watch what I do," and she begins counting the sections between pegs out loud. She counts 10 sections and says, "It's not the same perimeter because mine is only 8."

Mr. Jim extends the challenge for Leah: "Can you tell Monette how she should change her rectangle so that its perimeter will be 8 instead of 10?" Leah touches the pegs and explains, "Take the geoband off these two pegs and move it to these two pegs to make it shorter." Monette does this. Mr. Jim watches and responds: "Monette, you followed Leah's directions, so now you two have conquered the challenge!"

Mr. Jim could have helped Monette solve the problem by herself. Instead, he took in what each girl was doing and decided to extend their learning by guiding them to work together and learn from each other.

In each of these examples, the teacher made three decisions in order to help children learn — (1) what content to focus on, (2) what the child was ready to learn next, and (3) how to make learning meaningful by relating the child's new learning to what he or she was already doing and thinking about.

Ten Strategies for Extending Learning

In the pages that follow, you'll learn about 10 strategies that you can use to extend children's learning in a Powerful Interaction:

1. **Help Children See Themselves as Thinkers.** When you think aloud with children, you can extend their learning by encouraging them to tune in to their own thinking, think in new ways, put their thoughts into words, and appreciate the thinking of others. In turn, you'll grow more skilled at asking questions and posing challenges that support higher-order thinking.

2. **Respond to Curiosity.** Curiosity motivates children to learn and explore. When you see children being curious, it's a rich opportunity to encourage and extend their learning. Supporting children's curiosity will raise your own curiosity level and you'll be a strong learning model for children.

3. **Use Mirror Talk.** Providing children with feedback makes them feel that they are noticed and their work is valued. Reflecting back what you see and hear them doing can extend learning by helping children become aware of their actions and thinking. Using mirror talk also gives you time to carefully observe to see what a child knows and can do.

4. **Have Conversations.** Whether verbal or nonverbal, conversations strengthen relationships and at the same time can extend children's language awareness, understanding, and thinking. Conversations are also an enjoyable way for you to interact with and teach children.

5. **Inspire Imaginative Play.** Children's imaginative play develops their symbolic thinking — thinking about people, places, and things that aren't right there in front of them. In addition, you are practicing the valuable skill of perspective taking when you see the world through children's eyes, and you may rediscover the joy that comes from pretending!

6. **Solve Problems Together.** By collaborating with children, you can help them think through the steps of solving a problem, use multiple strategies, and develop a positive attitude toward problem solving. Collaborative problem solving with children will contribute to a strong sense of community in your classroom, which will make your work feel more fulfilling.

REALITY CHECK When you are just getting started with Powerful Interactions, it's easier to practice them with one child at a time. However, as they become more a part of how you teach, you'll discover that at times, you can have Powerful Interactions with more than one child at once.

7. Use Rich Vocabulary. The more complex and different words you use with children, the bigger their vocabularies grow! There's a strong relationship between children's vocabularies and their success in school, so this is a critical way to extend their learning. Not only will children's vocabularies grow, yours will, too!

8. Laugh with Children. When you bring humor into your interactions with children, you extend their learning by exposing them to new ways of thinking and playing with language. You also teach them life skills, such as how to get along with others, laugh together, and relieve stress. Adding more laughter and humor makes your classroom a nicer place to be, which can really reduce the stress level that often comes with working with young children.

9. Ask Questions. The right kind of questions asked in just the right way can achieve so much, including igniting children's curiosity and pushing them to think in new ways. Really skilled teachers have a wide repertoire of questions to rely on. The more you use this strategy, the larger your repertoire becomes and the more effective you'll be as a teacher.

10. Link the New to the Familiar. Helping children relate new concepts and information to what they already know and are interested in makes it more likely they'll remember and use what they learn. As you become more skilled at creating links for children, they'll begin to feel closer to you because you know them so well. With that closeness comes a greater desire to cooperate with you, making classroom life more manageable.

As you explore each of these strategies, you'll come to see the many ways they are interconnected and overlapping: You ask children questions as you solve problems with them. You use rich vocabulary as you have conversations with children. Just as we did with the strategies for Step Two, Connect, we've described each strategy separately so that you can gain a deeper understanding of each one.

Now let's explore the 10 strategies for Step Three, **Extend Learning.** ✳

Help Children See
Themselves as Thinkers

What was I **thinking?** Put on your **thinking** cap. **Think** it over. **Think** before you speak. Wishful **thinking!** I'm just **thinking** out loud. To my way of **thinking**… I can't **think** straight! Come to **think** of it… **Think** nothing of it. **Think** outside the box. **Thinking** on your feet. **Think** big! I **think** the world of you!

Call attention to children's thinking to help them become more aware of their own and others' thoughts and become more confident about expressing their thoughts.

Even though you may use the word *think* all the time, and your mind is always full of thoughts, have you ever stopped to really think about THINKING?

Stop for a moment and consider what thinking helps us to do. We think to
- Process language
- Solve problems
- Make choices
- Plan ahead
- Remember details
- Wish and dream
… What else?

Thinking with Children during Powerful Interactions

Focusing on thinking extends children's learning and can turn an everyday interaction into a Powerful Interaction. You help children see themselves as thinkers when you

- **Make them more aware of their own thinking.** Young children are usually aware of what their bodies are doing, but not aware of what's going on in their brains. Ask questions such as these:

  "What are you thinking about?"

  "What's going on in your mind?"

  "I wonder if you're thinking about your new kitten?"

- **Call attention to the thinking of others.** When you tell children about *your* thinking and encourage them to hear how other children think, they begin to learn that different people think in different ways.

  "Here's what I think."

  "Shall we find out what Francine thinks about that?"

  "I'll bet that we all have different thoughts about this story."

- **Invite them to explain their thinking out loud.** This helps them clarify the thoughts and ideas in their heads.

  "Tell me what you're thinking."

  "Explain your thinking, so we can understand your ideas."

- **Encourage them to think in new and different ways.** With your guidance, children's thinking can become more sophisticated and complex.

  "How would you describe that?"

  "How are these the same?"

  "How did you figure that out?"

  "What's another reason that could have happened?"

  "What do you believe about that?"

Here's Sheila's Powerful Interaction with 4-year-old Basanti. Watch and listen for ways the teacher focuses on thinking and how Basanti responds:

Sheila and Basanti are nestled together in a beanbag chair, looking at a counting book. On the page about the number 1, there is one object. On the page about the number 4, there are four sets of four objects, and so forth. As he turns to the page about the number 8, Basanti's face lights up.

Sheila: "Oh, my, Basanti, you look so excited. What are you thinking about?"

Basanti: "There's so many!" (He starts saying numbers very fast without pointing.) "One-two-three-four-five …"

Sheila: "Yes, eight is a pretty big quantity. We're going to have to really use our brains to count all eight of these sets. How do you think we should begin?"

Basanti: "I think we should go slow."

Sheila: "Why do you think we should count slowly?"

Basanti: "So we don't get mixed up."

Sheila: "So you think slow counting will help us be organized. That's good thinking, Basanti. I'm also thinking that we could use our fingers to help us."

Basanti: "Yeah, you do good thinking, too, Miss Sheila!"

What did you observe? How did Sheila help Basanti — Become more aware of his own thoughts? Become aware of *her* thinking? Explain his thinking out loud? Think in new or different ways?

REALITY

CHECK

There are many ways to think. One way is not better than another. Focusing on thinking is NOT about coming up with the "right" answer. The goal is to help children become more aware of the thoughts in their heads and more confident about expressing those thoughts to others. Avoid making thinking a competition to see who thinks the best!

Tips for Focusing on Thinking as You Interact

Here are some suggestions you can use to focus on thinking during Powerful Interactions.

Infuse the words *think* and *thinking* as you talk with the child.

"You look like you're thinking very hard." ... "Think about what you'd like to do on the playground today." ... "As I read this story, keep thinking about our trip to the farm yesterday."

Pose a direct question to invite the child to share his thoughts.

"What are you thinking about?" ... "I'm wondering what you're thinking. Would you like to share your idea?"

Use a gesture to indicate thinking, such as pointing to your forehead, looking up with your eyes, scratching your head, or resting your chin in your hand.

"Hmmm, I wonder what I can do with this blue block?" ... "That's a good question; let me give it some thought."

Before you ask a question that requires thinking, prepare the child.

"I'm going to ask you a question, so put on your thinking cap."

Give the child time to think before responding. Don't jump in too soon with the answer.

"How many is that? I'm going to give you a minute to think."

Help the child remember to think first before responding.

"Take another moment to think, and then let me know your thoughts."

Tell the child when you notice her thinking.

"I noticed that you had to think really hard to figure out how to put that puzzle together."

Share your thinking! Tell the child about your own thought processes.

"I was thinking about what story to read today, and I remembered how much you like Eric Carle's stories. So I asked myself, 'Are there any Eric Carle stories Amanda hasn't heard yet?' I thought about that question, and decided to read this one — *Rooster's Off to See the World*."

How's It Going?

As you focus on thinking in your Powerful Interactions with children, you may begin to notice that they're tuning in to their thinking more often and more independently. Keep your eyes and ears open for clues that your Powerful Interactions are having a positive impact on them and are extending their learning.

When children are thinking, you might notice them

- Imitating your thinking gestures, such as pointing to or scratching their heads

- Using the word *think* as they talk to each other

    "What do you think?" … "Good thinking!" … "Put on your thinking cap!"

- Growing more comfortable with and capable of explaining their thinking

    "I decided to draw it that way because it looks like the illustration in the book."

- Exclaiming about their own thinking

    "Hey, I thought about it and figured it out!"

Remember: *Children will think of themselves as thinkers if you teach them about thinking! Focusing on thinking during your Powerful Interactions is the most effective way to do this.*

Respond to Curiosity

Can you remember what you were curious about as a child? As an adult, what makes you stop, wonder, and investigate?

Notice children's curiosity about objects and events, and use it to guide and extend their learning.

Young Children Are Naturally Curious

When we are young, the whole world is new to us. During a child's early years, curiosity is stronger and more obvious than during any other period of life. You work with young children, so you do not have to look very hard or far to see it. Consider these examples:

Four-month-old Ramon lifts his head and looks in the direction of a ringing bell.

Nine-month-old Terri reaches for a plastic squeeze toy, picks it up, puts it in her mouth, and bites down on it. It squeaks and she giggles!

One-year-old Matthew climbs up on the sofa and peeks under a blanket to look for his teddy bear.

Eighteen-month-old Lancia bends down toward a flower and sniffs it.

Three-year-old Josiah spots a beetle during outside time and asks, "What's that?"

Four-year-old Felicity sees a bird at the birdfeeder and exclaims, "Hey, that big bird's going to eat all the seeds!"

Five-year-old Danté watches steam rise from the teakettle and asks, "Why does hot water make smoke?"

Six-year-old Adara loves horses and is learning how to draw them in more detail. Wondering how to make the horse look like it's running fast, she looks in the classroom library for a book with pictures of horses.

When children show their curiosity, they let you know that they're wondering about the world. It's as if they're saying, "I want to learn more about this." When you celebrate, encourage, and promote curiosity in children, you lay a foundation for them to be learners — both now and throughout their lives.

Curiosity as an Invitation for a Powerful Interaction

Throughout each day, children show you their curiosity. These are ripe moments to have a Powerful Interaction because children are motivated and eager to think and learn in that moment.

Think about the children in your setting. What are they curious about? Knowing what a child is curious about provides you with a starting point to extend that child's learning. Learning is most meaningful when it relates to the learner's strong interest or curiosity.

When you see children being curious, they are sending you an invitation to encourage and guide their learning through a Powerful Interaction. Using a child's curiosity and following the three steps of Powerful Interactions, you create the perfect condition for you to teach and the child to learn:

- **Be present.** When you notice a child's curiosity, take a breath and do a Me Check. Can you join the child's mood of interest and excitement to create a just-right fit?

- **Connect.** Let the child know that you notice and appreciate her curiosity. Use her curiosity to nourish your relationship with her.

- **Extend Learning.** Tune in to the child's interest and follow her lead. At the same time, decide how to stretch the child's learning just a little bit.

Tips for Responding to Curiosity

As you read these tips, consider what you already do. Choose one or two new ideas to try.

Tell the child what you see him doing, and use the words *curious* and *curiosity*. He will know that you value curiosity, as well as learn a new word.

> "You are curious about that noise, aren't you, Ramon? Let's find out what's making that bell ring!"

Take pleasure in the child's curiosity.

> "Oh, Terri, that was pretty funny. You put that toy in your mouth and made it squeak!"

Join the child in his curiosity and model your own.

> "I wonder where your teddy bear is, Matthew? You looked under the blanket. Where else could we look? Let's look behind the bookshelf!"

Help the child relate her discovery to prior experience or knowledge.

> "You're smelling that flower, Lancia! I'm going to smell it, too. Oooo, that's a sweet smell. Smell it again. What does it remind you of?"

Encourage the child to notice a few details.

> "Oh, Josiah, you found an insect! Let's look at it closely. What do you notice?" (Josiah points to the legs.) "Yes, I see legs, too." (He points to feelers.) "I wonder what the feelers are for?" (He says, "Black.") "Yes, it's all black. Let's look it up in the insect book when we go back inside."

To extend the child's curiosity, ask an open-ended question related to what the child is doing.

> "Felicity, why do you think that blue jay is going to eat more than his share of the seeds?" (Felicity explains her thinking.) "If your prediction is right and he does eat all the seeds, what should we do?"

Help the child find answers to his questions, rather than answer them yourself.

> "That's a great question, Danté! How can you find out? … You think your mother might know? Shall I help you write it down so you won't forget to ask her tonight?"

REALITY

Extending children's learning in a Powerful Interaction does not have to take a lot of time. These exchanges were brief and powerful!

CHECK

How's It Going?

As you develop the habit of using children's curiosity as the basis for extending their learning in a Powerful Interaction, you may begin to notice some beneficial changes. When you see these changes happening around you, you'll know you are having a positive impact on children and extending their learning.

When you are fostering children's curiosity, you might notice them

- Being more curious than ever
- Using the words *curiosity* and *curious* as they talk about themselves ("I'm curious about this") or while talking with each other ("Are you curious?")
- Improving their observation skills, examining objects more closely and noticing more details

As you place more value on children's curiosity, you might notice

- You're more alert to children's curiosity
- Your own curiosity is reawakened and you're finding new ways to share it with children

Remember: *Curiosity is natural, so take advantage of it in your teaching. Curiosity is contagious, so allow yourself to "catch it." Curiosity is a necessary ingredient for learning, so nurture it in children!*

Use Mirror Talk

"As you write your name, I can see that you are going slowly and trying to make each letter the same size."

Think of a time when you walked into a situation and weren't quite sure what to say. Perhaps you

- Blurted out the wrong thing at the wrong time
- Hurt someone's feelings because you didn't notice their work or effort
- Talked and talked without saying anything meaningful

As you notice the things children are doing as they work and play, give them feedback by telling them what you see and hear them doing.

Listen as teachers describe something similar that happened to them when they joined a child in an interaction not knowing what to say.

- *It's so hard to break the habit of saying stuff like, "You're doing a great job cleaning up, David!"*
- *I know I shouldn't ask so many quizzing questions. And the quieter the child, the more quiz questions I ask. When Eden was at the computer, I must have fired five questions at her.*
- *I can see she's using red paint and I know that she knows the color red. But what comes right out of my mouth, "What color paint are you using, Cherelle?"*

How Mirror Talk Supports Learning

Talking with children, especially giving them feedback, as they work and play can extend their thinking and learning. But sometimes it's hard to know what to say to be most effective for that child at that moment. Other times we know what we should say, but can't help acting on bad habits.

In the examples above, what David's, Eden's, and Cherelle's teachers said to them wasn't particularly harmful, but it wasn't very helpful either. Such comments and questions do little to advance your relationship with a child or to extend that child's development and learning.

Let's look at how a strategy called *mirror talk* is an alternative and more effective way to give children feedback.

Using mirror talk with a child means simply reflecting back to the child what you see or hear him doing or saying. Consider what you could have said in the same situations as the examples above:

> You observe David cleaning up in the dramatic play area. Instead of general praise, you might say, "You're making everything neat and tidy in here, David."

> You see Eden using the story program at the computer. Instead of firing questions at her you say, "Eden, I see you're up to the part of the story where the bears go for a walk."

> You see Cherelle painting at the easel. Instead of asking an obvious question, you might say, "Look at that picture you're painting, Cherelle. You've used four different colors!"

Mirror talk nurtures your relationships with children because you are noticing them and letting them know that you value what they are doing. Mirror talk also supports children's learning because it gives them specific, detailed information about what they are doing and saying. This feedback helps children become more aware of their own thinking and learning. That, in turn, encourages them to repeat, practice, and build on the behaviors that contribute to learning (and to reduce or change behaviors that don't).

In other words, by recognizing and telling children about the actions and language that you want to promote, you motivate them to repeat those actions and practice that language. Thus, their skills develop and improve.

DID YOU KNOW? If you use mirror talk when you observe children being kind, patient, cooperative, diligent, and otherwise behaving appropriately, children will know that you value those behaviors, and less acceptable behaviors are likely to diminish.

Giving Mirror Talk a Try

**Here's Natalie. What is she doing?
What could you say to her?**

Perhaps you come over and say, "Natalie, you're so busy putting soil in the plant pot, just like a gardener getting ready to plant seeds."

Now think about Natalie's perspective. What effect might your mirror talk have on her?

- She might feel good because you noticed what she's doing.
- She might think, "Oh, this brown stuff is called soil. And this thing is called a plant pot!"
- Perhaps she hadn't really thought about what she'd do next. But now she is thinking about the next step — planting seeds.
- Maybe she was beginning to lose interest in this activity; but because you're interested and curious, she decides to stick with it.

By using mirror talk, you connect with Natalie, activating the safety and trust she feels when she's with you. At the same time, you support and extend her learning in several ways: by focusing her attention and making her aware of her actions, introducing new vocabulary, giving her something new to think about, encouraging her engagement, and more. You and Natalie had a Powerful Interaction!

Hooray for Mirror Talk!

When a child expresses pride or excitement in what she is doing, you want to mirror her emotions and share her celebratory mood. To do that, add expressions such as "Wow!" … "Oh my" … "Hooray!" … "Look at you" … "Cool" … "High five!" … and "Congratulations" to your mirror talk. Acknowledging the child's own sense of success affirms her feelings of competence. Doing this is different from giving general praise such as "Good job," which only reinforces the empty goal of pleasing the teacher.

Another Mirror Talk Example

Listen in on Gina as she uses mirror talk to have a Powerful Interaction with 9-month-old Teddy, who is playing with his rubber ducky.

Teddy lies on his back on the carpet. With both hands, he holds onto a squishy duck-shaped squeeze toy that is sitting on his belly. Gina approaches and kneels on the floor beside him.

Gina: "Teddy, you're holding that rubber ducky tight in your hands!" (Teddy lifts the rubber duck up in the air and looks at it.)

Gina: "There! Now you can see that funny little duck!"

Teddy waves the toy around in the air a little bit.

Gina: "Oh, look, you can make the duck fly! I wonder what will happen if you squeeze it."

Gina reaches over, gently places her hand on top of Teddy's hands and gives the toy a squeeze. It squeaks. Teddy looks surprised, and they both laugh.

In Gina's Powerful Interaction with Teddy, she strengthens her relationship with him by giving him meaningful attention. And, she extends his thinking and learning by introducing him to some wonderful new language and cause-and-effect thinking!

Tips for Using Mirror Talk

Notice the things children do and say, and reflect that back to them.
To use this strategy during Powerful Interactions is simple. For example, when you see

- A baby reach for a rattle:

  "Wow, you really stretched your arm to get that rattle!"

- A toddler pick up a pebble from the ground and look at it:

  "Oh, my! You found a very interesting pebble. Feel how smooth it is!"

- A 3-year-old stacking blocks and saying, "Hooray, I can do it!"

  "Hooray for you! You're stacking the blocks one on top of the other to make a tower. I wonder if you can build it even higher!"

- A 4-year-old take her coat off and hang it on a hook:

  "Look at you! You can take off your coat and hang it up. I remember when that was hard for you to do!"

- A 5-year-old place a leaf under the tripod magnifier:

  "I see you're using the magnifying lens to investigate the details of the leaf. What do you notice?"

- A 6-year-old using tally marks to keep score of a card game and announcing, "I figured out this cool way to keep score!"

  "Using tally marks is a pretty cool way to keep score! How did you figure out how to do that?"

DID YOU KNOW? You don't have to wait for a child to do something amazing! Mirror talk works just fine for the ordinary, everyday things children do — rolling over, crawling, walking, skipping, jumping, hopping, climbing, babbling, talking, singing, eating, giggling, drawing, painting, and building! Watch to see how positively children respond to your feedback.

I've been using mirror talk with my 4-year-olds for a while and now they're using it with each other. I hear them saying, "I notice that. ..." They are really looking at each other's work and taking time to tell each other what they see.

— Kim (a preschool teacher)

How's It Going?

Teachers who use mirror talk discover it produces a variety of positive effects. You, too, may begin to see small changes happening around you as your feedback has a positive impact on children and extends their learning.

Children are apt to start responding in new ways to your use of mirror talk. They might

- Shift from staring at you to smiling, babbling, repeating what you said, inviting you to play, or telling you a story
- Initiate more interactions with you by telling you what they're doing
- Begin using mirror talk themselves

The climate of your teaching space also might begin shifting. It might

- Feel calmer because children aren't clamoring for your praise and approval
- Take on a slower pace as children stay involved in what they're doing for longer periods of time
- Become more pleasant because the things children do take on more meaning

You might change, too. You might

- Grow more relaxed about approaching children as they work and play
- Find the things children do and say more interesting
- Focus more on the positive things that children with challenging behaviors do and say
- Feel more effective as a teacher because you're immediately using what you observe to guide children's learning

Remember: *You make a difference and mirror talk can help! When you use mirror talk, you'll help children feel comfortable and confident. And you'll also nudge their learning forward.*

Have Conversations

Imagine you're heading out to have lunch with a good friend you haven't seen or talked with for a year. You're really looking forward to the conversation. Thoughts start swirling around in your mind:

- I wonder what we'll talk about this time?

- What do I want to share?

- What do I want to ask her about?

- What will the surprise topic be this time? Our conversations always have surprises. That's one reason I love them!

In your verbal and nonverbal interactions with children, really listen to learn what children know and how they are thinking, and gently stretch them to think about new ideas and new topics.

What is it about conversations with certain people that make them so enjoyable and gratifying? Perhaps it's the feeling of partnership and companionship. Or maybe it's the excitement of seeing where the conversation will lead. ... Or the possibility of learning something new.

Conversations during Powerful Interactions with Children

Learning is a social process. We learn when we watch and listen to others. Each time we play, work, and talk with others, we learn — new ideas, new words, and new skills. Through conversations, even nonverbal ones, we relate, communicate, and learn from one another. We interact!

You can learn a lot about what children know and how they think in your back-and-forth exchanges with them. Conversations not only strengthen your relationships with children, they also allow you to extend children's learning — their language, thinking, understanding of ideas, and awareness of the world.

As you read this story about Lucy and 18-month-old Sophia, see if you can detect what Lucy says and does to turn her conversation with Sophia into a Powerful Interaction.

Sophia is sitting on the floor of the library area, stacking board books on top of each other. Her teacher, Lucy, sits down by her side.

"I haven't checked in with Sophia this morning. Let's see what's happening here."

After a minute or two, Lucy decides to interact.

Lucy: "Sophia, look at the stack of board books you're making. I wonder which one you'll choose to read."

"I'll use mirror talk and then share my curiosity."

Sophia keeps on stacking. Lucy thinks about what to say or do next.

Sophia takes two books from the pile — *Goodnight Moon* and *Yoo-hoo, Little Rabbit!* — and pushes them in front of Lucy.

"Mmm... I want to ask her which book she'd like me to read, but maybe I'll keep my mouth closed for a bit and just see what happens."

Lucy: "You chose two books, Sophia."

Sophia smiles with delight and uses both index fingers to point to the books.

Sophia: "Bunnies!"

"Perhaps Sophia is taking the lead. I'll follow."

Matching Sophia's smile, Lucy grins, too.

Lucy: "Sophia, you found two books with bunnies on their covers! We can play a game!"

Sophia giggles. Lucy finds two books with puppies on the covers and gives them to Sophia, who places them beside the bunny books and points with both index fingers.

Sophia: "Puppies!"

"Now that's a surprise! She found two books with pictures of rabbits on the cover. I wonder if she can see similarities between other books."

Think about how Lucy uses conversation (verbal and nonverbal) to connect with Sophia and then to extend Sophia's learning. What does she say and do to

- Get the conversation going?
- Keep it going back and forth multiple times?
- Follow Sophia's lead?
- Extend Sophia's learning?

Now think about your verbal and nonverbal conversations with the individual children in your group. Consider these questions (your answers may vary depending on the child):

- How do you initiate conversations with those children?
- How many times does your conversation usually go back and forth?
- What are some ways you keep your conversations going?
- Who controls the direction your conversations take? You? The child? Both of you?

Tips for Extending Learning in Conversations

Conversations with children become Powerful Interactions when you take the time to be present and connect with them. To be effective,

Be a good listener, showing respect and appreciation for the child's verbal and nonverbal contributions.

Use interesting language and vocabulary. Avoid baby talk. Don't worry about simplifying your language. Talk in a normal, conversational manner.

Repeat and clarify what the child says. Avoid overtly correcting the child's pronunciation and grammar. Instead, simply rephrase or reword correctly what the child said.

When Kimberly says "telebishon" her teacher says, "Oh, you watched television last night?" Kimberly smiles and says, "Yes."

Use open-ended prompts to keep the conversation going.

"Tell me more about that." … "Really? What happened next?" … "What else did you see?"

Talk about topics that are interesting to the child.

"You went to the pool? That sounds like fun!" … "Did your dog have her puppies yet?"

Encourage conversations between children. Let children know you value their conversations with each other.

"You two were having a long conversation about soccer during snack today!"

Invite another child to join your one-to-one conversation.

"Tommy, Phillip and I are talking about our favorite kinds of ice cream. I wonder if yours are the same or different from ours."

Introduce "talking partners" into group discussions.

"Talk about this with your talking partner. Make sure you hear each other's ideas."

How's It Going?

As you sharpen your conversation skills during Powerful Interactions, look for clues that you are having a positive impact on children and extending their learning. You'll know you are making a difference when you see any of these changes happening.

Children might be

- Initiating and leading more conversations: "Hey, Ms. Debbie, I saw the moon last night! Did you?"
- Taking a more active role in conversations
- Engaging in longer conversations
- Talking about a wider range of topics
- Having conversations with each other: "I have an apple for snack. What do you have?"

Families might be

● Sharing conversations they've had with their child

You might be

● Realizing that conversations with children are the high points of your day

REALITY **CHECK** *Try to avoid bombarding children with questions. They'll shut down under the attack, and your conversation will end.*

Remember: *Back-and-forth exchanges (conversations) are a common and important ingredient of Powerful Interactions. Stay open to both verbal and nonverbal ways to keep the conversation going. Conversations that gently stretch the child to think and talk about new topics and consider new points of view are powerful ways to extend learning.*

Inspire Imaginative Play

As a teacher, you have the privilege of watching children's imaginative play every day. Can you picture these examples?

> Malika, 30 months, moves small plastic animals in and out of a small barn, making a different animal noise for each one.

> Xavier and Warren, both 4-year-olds, wear hard hats and create roads and tunnels in the sandbox.

> Six-year-old Lizzy puts a bonnet on her head and a basket over her arm and acts out a scene from *Little House on the Prairie*.

What do you notice when children are engaged in such play? Total interest and absorption? Cooperation with others? Rich language?

As you get involved in children's play, reflect their language and actions back to them, introduce new ideas, and steer them in appropriate directions.

Using Imaginative Play to Extend Learning

When children are about 2 years old, they begin to recall experiences, remember details, and create images in their minds. As they play, they tap into their memories, re-create their experiences, and pretend to be other people, in other places, and in other times.

Imaginative play comes naturally to young children and it gives them great pleasure. And, imaginative play is crucial to the development of children's thinking and learning. When they use their imaginations, children think about people, places, and things that aren't right there in front of them. This is called *abstract* or *symbolic* thinking.

For example, after visiting a veterinarian, a child stores those sights, sounds, and smells in her brain. When the child returns to the classroom, she recalls these memories as she acts out the role of a vet in the dramatic play area. She pretends to use the tools, language, and procedures that the real vet used. In this way, imaginative play is a form of exercise for the brain.

Moreover, when young children engage in imaginative play, they practice picturing things in their minds. This symbolic thinking lays the groundwork for later learning in reading, writing, and math.

- As children engage in pretend play, they make up stories. As their play gets more sophisticated, they create a setting, characters, dialogue, beginnings, and endings. This is great practice for reading or writing stories with the same features.

- To understand what they are reading, children have to be able to see a picture of what each word stands for in their minds.

- To solve math problems, such as adding three oranges and seven apples, children have to picture them in their minds.

DID YOU KNOW? Research shows a link between "intentional make-believe play" and the development of cognitive and social skills that are prerequisites for learning more complex concepts. For example, such play is linked to growth in memory, self-regulation, oral language, and recognizing symbols. It has been linked to higher levels of school adjustment and increased social development. Such play has also been linked to increased literacy skills and other areas of academic learning.

(Bodrova & Leong 2007)

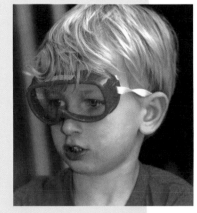

Powerful Interactions during Imaginative Play

Children's imaginative play is a wonderful setting for Powerful Interactions. When you engage with children in imaginative play, you learn what they know about their world. As you begin to see the world through their eyes and join them in their play, a very personal connection grows. Imaginative play offers a relaxed setting in which relationships can flourish and grow. And in the security of those relationships, you have a rich opportunity to extend children's learning in small steps.

Ms. Kahn runs a small child care program in her home. Let's watch as she enters 5-year-old Taro's imaginative play:

> Outside time is coming to an end. Ms. Kahn gathers the last few children to come inside for snack. Most are already inside with the assistant. Ms. Kahn is not surprised to see that one of the remaining children is Taro. He is slow to make transitions and it's easy for her to get impatient with him. Today she feels like she has a few extra minutes to have a Powerful Interaction with him rather than a power struggle. She looks over to see Taro perched atop the jungle gym. He's wearing a floppy hat that he brought from the collection of dress-up clothes inside. He holds a small stick he found on the ground in one hand. He holds his other hand across his forehead, as if he's searching the horizon for something.
>
> **Taro:** "Ahoy there, mate! Are you friend or foe? This is the great ship Landlubber and we are armed!"
>
> **Ms. Kahn:** "Ahoy there, mate, Pirate Taro! I'm a friend, so Landlubber's arms can remain silent."
>
> **Taro:** "How do I know for sure you're a friend?"
>
> **Ms. Kahn:** "Here comes Pirate Lara. She'll vouch for me. Pirate Lara, tell Pirate Taro that I'm not an enemy and that I come with a peaceful invitation."
>
> **Lara:** "She's okay, Pirate Taro!"
>
> **Taro:** "Okay, you must prove you're a friend. What's your peaceful invitation?"
>
> **Ms. Kahn:** (pretending to pull a letter out of her back pocket) "I come to you with an invitation from the leader of this land to join me at the table for milk and special pirate cookies!"
>
> **Taro:** "What makes them pirate cookies?"
>
> **Ms. Kahn:** "Oh, they are full of treasures from a sunken shipwreck! You won't believe how delicious they are!"
>
> **Taro:** "Okay, Ms. Kahn, I'll take one more look around and then I'll come."

What do you think? Did Ms. Kahn reach her goal of having a Powerful Interaction with Taro?

- **What did she do to be present?** She paused and did a Me Check. She acknowledged that she and Taro often get into power struggles at transition times, and she consciously decided to take the Powerful Interaction route this time.

- **Did she take the connect step?** She made a strong personal connection with Taro by entering his imaginative play world rather than staying outside its boundaries. She nurtured their relationship by playing pirate along with him.

- **What did she do to extend learning?** After re-establishing a positive connection with Taro, Ms. Kahn stretched his play and exposed him to some colorful and sophisticated vocabulary — "vouch," "peaceful invitation," "leader of the land," and "sunken shipwreck," to name a few.

Ms. Kahn's Powerful Interaction with Taro illustrates your role in children's imaginative play. Many teachers wonder what their role should be. Fearing that they'll disrupt the play by joining in, some watch from afar and don't get involved. Others want so much to be "The Teacher" that they join the play and begin asking lots of questions: "Where are you going all dressed up like that?" … "What color paint are you using?" … "How many animals are in your barn?" These quiz-type questions are often disruptive to children's imaginative play.

Ms. Kahn joined Taro's play, but she didn't take over. She steered the direction of the play, but made sure that Taro maintained his sense of control. By assuming the role of pirate and involving another child as a third pirate, she added complexity and depth to his imaginative play, which was already at quite a high level.

> *"This year, I have a group of children who are fantastic actors! They pretend from the beginning of the day to the end. They've made me into an actor, too! And now I realize I can have a big 'teaching' impact by joining their dramatic play, not just watching it. Teaching has never been more fun!"*
>
> *— LaTanya (a kindergarten teacher)*

Tips for Inspiring Imagination

We encourage you to try Ms. Kahn's approach. Here are some tips.

Be a player. Pull up a chair, get down on the floor, put on a hat, listen to the story, play the game. You'll connect with the child and communicate some important messages: "You are doing something interesting." … "I like you!" … "I want to be part of what you are doing."

Be a mirror. Let children know you see and hear them. Reflect their actions and language back to them:

"You look so grown-up wearing those big shoes and carrying that pocketbook!"

"That baby looks very comfy in the cradle. You gave him a pillow, a bottle, and his blanky!"

"I see two carpenters at work in the block area. You've got lots of tools. I think you must have a big job to do."

"I see that the famous artist has donned her smock. It looks like she's ready to produce another masterpiece!"

Be a rubber band. Stretch the child's play a little bit:

Introduce another prop: "You know, we have a tutu in the classroom. Would you like to wear it as you dance?"

Use some interesting language: "You're illustrating your story with your painting."

Add a new idea: "Come here little puppy. I have a treat for you, but you have to do a trick! Can you beg? Sit up? Roll over? Play dead?"

REALITY
CHECK

You may find that joining children's play feels awkward. Don't give up. Recall childhood memories of using your imagination. Don't worry if some of your interactions don't feel like Powerful Interactions at first. Keep trying!

Be a steering wheel. When the imaginative play goes in a direction that might not be appropriate, take on a role that allows you redirect the play in a more appropriate direction:

> "Oh, my, Teddy doesn't know about manners, does he? We'll have to teach him the polite way to say that. Do you want to teach him or should I?"

> "Lady lion, you're roaring so loudly. Are you upset about something? Whisper in my ear and then I'll see if the zookeeper has any more lion treats!"

> "Dr. Michael, you made poisons for the people to drink? Are they sick? Do they need to go to the hospital? Why don't you call an ambulance and I'll make sure they're okay."

How's It Going?

Joining children's imaginative play helps you to connect with children so you can deepen your relationship and extend their learning. These Powerful Interactions are also great fun! As you play, watch for clues that you're using this strategy effectively. Here are some clues to look for.

- You're increasingly comfortable with your role as a supporting actor rather than a director.
- Children's imaginative play episodes are getting longer, more children are involved, and they need less outside support to stay engaged.
- You find it easier to model interesting language when you join the play.
- Families tell you more stories and ask more questions about their children's imaginative play at home.
- Children imitate your gestures, facial expressions, voice inflections, and actions.
- The stories children develop through their imaginative play throughout the classroom are more complex:
  - Plots have more twists and turns.
  - Children are taking on more diverse roles in their play.
  - Children use a wider variety of props.

Remember: *By inspiring children to use their imaginations in new ways during a Powerful Interaction, you help them to expand their pretend skills, which in turn extends their abstract/symbolic thinking.*

Solve Problems Together

Think about a "problem" you solved recently. Perhaps it was figuring out how to get your two daughters to different events across town on the same day and time. Or how to assemble the bookshelf you bought at Ikea. Did you find a solution? Which traits or skills helped you succeed? Which interfered?

Help children learn the attitudes and skills they need to confidently solve problems by modeling problem solving and helping children learn how to think through the steps to a solution.

For young children, everything is new and every day presents fresh experiences, challenges, and puzzles to be explored, understood, and solved:

- "How do I get the applesauce in this bowl into my mouth?"
- "I've dumped the blocks onto the floor, but now what?"
- "I want to wear the firefighter hat because I'm the Fire Chief! You wore it yesterday ... that's not fair!"

When you see children solving problems, you have a golden opportunity for a Powerful Interaction.

Solving Problems to Extend Learning

As you interact with children, you can help them develop a positive attitude toward solving problems and learn how to think through the steps that lead to a solution. Children will use these problem-solving skills throughout their lifetimes.

Many children are naturally enthusiastic, persistent, and patient problem solvers. Some approach problems without a plan and need guidance to be more systematic. You may observe that others approach problems with fear, resistance, or an "I can't" attitude. With your support and encouragement during Powerful Interactions, children can unlearn negative messages about problem solving and gain positive ones!

As you interact with children, be a problem solver, model, and guide. Let's take a look at the attitudes and skills children need to learn:

● **Being curious and persistent.** Curiosity motivates us to see problems and have the eagerness to tackle them. Persistence enables us to stay with a problem until it is solved or resolved. Here are some ways you model and teach curiosity and persistence:

As a baby tries over and over to get the rattle into her mouth, watch patiently with a smile on your face. Or, you might use mirror talk: "I can see how hard you are trying to get the rattle into your mouth."

Show toddlers lots of ways to play with a ball — rolling, bouncing, throwing.

As preschoolers try to make the baby doll stop crying, encourage them to try different ways (patting its back, feeding, rocking, calling the doctor).

Use the words *curious* and *persistent* with kindergartners as they use recycled materials to "invent" a computer.

● **Identifying and defining the problem.** Good problem solvers know when they have a problem and can describe it. You model and teach children how to identify and define a problem when you

Say to a baby who has pulled her hat off: "That hat is a problem for you. You don't want it on your head. It doesn't feel good, does it?"

Tell a toddler as he gets up from naptime: "Your shoe is giving you a problem! It's hard to get it on your foot, isn't it?"

Talk to a preschooler who struggles at snack time: "Those darn juice boxes! Opening them up gives everyone a problem."

Speak to kindergartners arguing about the score in a game: "Keeping track of points for four different people is a difficult problem to solve. Let's think about how we might do that."

- **Having multiple strategies.** Problem solvers have a repertoire of approaches to try and can think flexibly about which one might work best in each situation. You can model and teach basic problem-solving strategies:

  Brainstorming: "Let's brainstorm lots of different ways we could solve this problem."

  Trial and error: "I just watched you try four different ways to solve that problem! That's called trial and error."

  Applying prior knowledge: "I remember that you had a problem like this last week. What did you try that time? Maybe that strategy will work for this problem, too."

  Trying alternatives: "Maybe you could solve this problem by using a different tool."

  Getting help: "Who could help us solve this problem? Maybe we have a book that would give us the information we need."

- **Analyzing and evaluating.** After possible solutions are identified, problem solvers analyze and evaluate them to decide which one to try first. You can model and teach analysis and evaluation by thinking aloud with children of all ages:

"It's chilly outside. We could wrap up in blankets, but then we wouldn't be able to play. I think jackets will work better."

"We don't have quite enough apples for everyone. I thought about having two different snacks, but I decided to cut these apples into smaller pieces to share, so everyone would have the same snack."

"I picked out three different stories to read today, and I couldn't decide which one to read. Then I remembered that you were interested in the ants on the playground the other day, so I chose this one, *Two Bad Ants*."

- **Reflecting.** After finding a solution to a problem, good problem solvers think a little more. They go back over what happened and reflect on how well their strategy or solution worked. You can model and teach how to reflect on the solutions to problems by asking questions like these:

  "What was easy about solving that problem? What was hard?"

  "How did that solution work out for you?"

  "Why do you think that solution worked (or didn't work) so well?"

  "What do you think you'll try the next time you run into a problem like that?"

Modeling and Teaching Problem Solving during Powerful Interactions

Using the steps of Powerful Interactions as you solve problems together with children will help them become more confident and competent problem solvers.

- **Pause to be present.** By first doing a Me Check, you can decide if this is a good moment to support the child in problem solving and whether you are in the right frame of mind. If you decide to go forward, then you can focus on individual children, appreciate the problems they're working on, and scaffold them in a deliberate way that fits each child and situation.

REALITY CHECK Helping Children to Solve Problems

Many adults have a hard time watching a young child struggle with a problem, and often they move in to solve the problem for the child. However, when you take an active role in offering children interesting problems to solve and join them in the process of solving them, you'll be making meaningful connections with children and helping them move forward as thinkers.

- **Connect to deepen your relationship.** When you do and say things that remind children of the trust and comfort they feel when they're with you, they feel more confident and relaxed. Then, they can give a full measure of concentration to solving the problem at hand.

- **Extend learning.** Problem solving is a lifelong learning skill. As you help children develop the problem-solving attitudes and skills identified above, you are making a difference!

Tips for Solving Problems with Children

Here are some suggestions you can use to turn everyday interactions into Powerful Interactions with children as they solve problems:

Use the word *problem*. When you notice a child tackling a challenging problem, use mirror talk — that is, say what you see or hear.

> "Thela, you are really stretching and reaching for that toy. You are determined to solve that problem!"

> "Armon, you're trying to figure out how to draw a cat. That's an interesting problem to solve. Shall we work on it together?"

Take advantage of everyday problems. Invite children to brainstorm solutions and solve everyday problems with you — for example, not enough napkins for snack time, running out of a certain color paint, a broken faucet, arguments about the rules of a game, a torn page in a book, a lost item, a big mess to clean up, an uncooperative person.

Offer interesting problems to solve. Give children challenges to tackle — for example, an attention-grabbing object just out of reach; containers with different kinds of latches; a variety of objects to roll down a ramp; a collection of shells to sort in as many ways as possible; the task of building something they've never tried before; finding objects other than brushes to paint with at the easel.

Use problem-solving vocabulary. When you use words such as *challenge*, *strategy*, *solution*, *brainstorm*, *experiment*, *test*, and *trial and error*, children will begin to use these words, as well.

 REALITY *You do not have to turn every problem into a Powerful Interaction. Sometimes, in the interest of safety or to protect a child's feelings, a problem needs to be solved quickly by you or with your help. In these situations, try to involve the child or* **CHECK** *children in a supportive discussion afterwards.*

How's It Going?

Watch to see how Powerful Interactions that include problem solving are making a difference. Are children beginning to internalize and apply what you've taught them about solving problems? Have your own classroom practices changed? Do you sense a change in your classroom climate? You might notice some of these things:

- Children are asking you and their friends for help solving problems.
- Children are happy and proud when they solve problems: "Hey, I solved a problem!" … "I figured out how this works!"
- Children are beginning to suggest solutions to problems during group discussions.
- You are helping children solve problems, rather than solving problems for them.
- You are validating children's efforts at solving problems: "You didn't give up. You came up with a good solution to that problem!"
- Family members are telling you stories about how their children are solving problems at home: "Last night I commented that the noodles were hot. My toddler told me to blow on them!"

Remember: *Pausing to be present and connecting with a child to deepen your relationship makes it possible for you to get a handle on the problem a child is struggling with. Then, you can decide what to do and say to turn solving the problem into a Powerful Interaction!*

Use Rich Vocabulary

Where would you be without words? ... You couldn't say "Hello" or "Nice to see you." Or get what you need. Or thank someone for a kind gesture. Your feelings would stay buried inside.

As you read and talk with children, use many different and interesting words.

You'd stay lost if you couldn't ask for directions. And when the day ends, how would you say goodnight? Whether spoken or written or signed, the words that you understand when you hear or see them (your *receptive* vocabulary) and the words you use to communicate (your *expressive* vocabulary) allow you to function every day.

Using Rich Vocabulary to Extend Learning

As young children are spoken and read to by the people they care about, and then as they themselves converse and begin to read, their vocabularies grow at an astonishing rate: hundreds of words by preschool age and several thousand by first grade (Hart & Risley 1995).

Here's why it's so important for children to develop large vocabularies:

- Vocabulary knowledge directly impacts how well children learn to read. (Beck et al. 2002)

- The larger a child's vocabulary is at age 3, the more the child will comprehend what he reads by age 8. (Hart & Risley 1995)

- Vocabulary is at the heart of how well children understand what people say, what they understand about math, science, and social studies, and the degree to which they comprehend what they read. (Hirsch 2003)

Adding new and interesting words to your Powerful Interactions with children can be fun and enjoyable. At the same time you extend their learning by building their vocabulary. Listen as these three teachers stretch children's language:

Katanya joins 16-month-old Ian as he plays with a mixture of cornstarch and water: "Oh, Ian, you're scooping up this gooey mixture in your hands. Look at it drip and drizzle through your fingers. When you hold your hands up high, it takes more time to plop, plop onto the tray!"

———————

Mr. Lance and 3-year-old Jocelyn are building a tower together with blocks:

Jocelyn: "Look, Mr. Lance, it's getting tippy!"

Mr. Lance: "Uh-oh, it must be crooked and unbalanced. Can you straighten it out?"

Jocelyn: "It might fall."

Mr. Lance: "Don't worry. If it collapses, we can just rebuild it!"

———————

DID YOU KNOW?

Researchers Betty Hart and Todd Risley (1995) found that the number of different words children hear before their third birthdays has a huge impact on how well they do in school later on.

Five-year-old Petra is wandering by herself on the playground. Ms. Hillary decides to join her:

Ms. Hillary: "Hey, Petra, can I accompany you on your little hike around the playground?"

Petra: "I'm lookin' for bugs and I can't find any."

Ms. Hillary: "Okay, let's be entomologists together and find some insects to study! Where have you searched already?"

Petra: "I've searched by the slide and by the swings."

Ms. Hillary: "Well, let's think. If you were an insect, what would you like for your habitat — maybe some trees and tall grasses?"

Petra: "Yeah, let's go look by the apple tree. That would be a good havitat!"

Ms. Hillary: "I agree, that would be a fine insect habitat. Let's check it out!"

Because these teachers simultaneously create a relationship bond and extend learning in their Powerful Interactions, Ian, Jocelyn, and Petra are more likely to use these new vocabulary words.

Tips for Adding Rich Vocabulary to Your Interactions

Here are some suggestions you could use to build children's vocabularies during Powerful Interactions:

Put up lists. Hang lists of attention-grabbing words in different parts of your learning space.

Read aloud! Reading picture books with challenging, colorful words is a great way to build children's vocabularies. A few suggestions to get you started:

- *Sylvester and the Magic Pebble* (William Steig)
- *The Big Orange Splot* (Daniel Pinkwater)
- *Epossumondas* (Coleen Salley)
- *In the Land of Words: New and Selected Poems* (Eloise Greenfield)

Build your own vocabulary! Do crossword, find-a-word, and jumble puzzles; brainstorm words with colleagues in staff meetings; and learn a few words in children's home languages.

Give hints. To help children understand unfamiliar words, use visual clues, gestures, and facial expressions.

Converse, converse, converse! A culture of conversation will go a long way toward building children's vocabularies. Use the word *conversation* with children. Encourage children's conversations with each other; for example, tell them, "While we have snack, you can have a conversation with the person next to you." Post topics for good conversations on the wall as a reminder.

Create a world of words. Sing songs and recite poems with children. Talk about new words as they come up in conversations and books. Make "word-for-the-day" part of the daily routine. Post a sign in the library area: "Interesting Words We've Found in Books." Add the job of "vocabulary builder" to the roster of classroom jobs. When children ask about a particular word, build on their curiosity:

> "You're curious about that word, aren't you? I'll read that part again. Do you have any guesses about what it means?"

How's It Going?

Stay alert to clues that your efforts to use rich vocabulary in your Powerful Interactions are paying off. You'll know you are having a positive impact on children and extending their learning

When children

- Are using some of the same rich vocabulary you've been modeling
- Ask "What's that word mean?" as you read stories
- Are coming up with words for word lists on the walls

When you

- Are more aware of the words in the stories you read to children and are bringing them to children's attention more often
- Enjoy coming up with interesting words to use, and find yourself using empty words such as *stuff* and *thing* much less often

When family members

- Tell you about new words they hear their child using at home

MORE WORD IDEAS
Check out the article by Holly Seplocha and Janis Strasser: "Using Fanciful, Magical Language in Preschool" in the April/May 2009 issue of *Teaching Young Children*. (Online: www.naeyc.org/files/tyc/file/FancifulLanguage.pdf)

Remember: *When you use a rich vocabulary, you not only teach children new words and extend their thinking. You also show them the pleasure of language that can lead to learning for the rest of their lives.*

REALITY

CHECK

Children learning English as a second language will need extra vocabulary help during Powerful Interactions. To give them support with rich vocabulary, you can act out words, use gestures, show children real objects or pictures, and say words in both languages.

Laugh with Children!

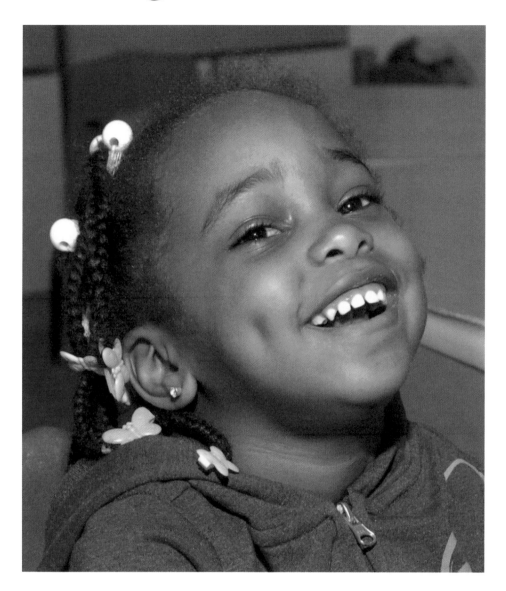

Imagine yourself in your classroom and tune in to the sounds of children. Hear their laughter, giggles, and chuckles. Feel their sense of hilarity, joy, and glee. Think about the children in your program. What makes them laugh?

Look for playful ways to interact with children — sing silly songs, read funny books and rhymes, and redirect challenging behavior with humor.

When it comes to laughter, playfulness, and silliness, children are the ultimate professionals! Young children find things to laugh about at every turn.

Humor and Powerful Interactions

Laughter, silliness, and playfulness can help to make your interactions with children powerful. When you take a moment to be present, and then connect, you're likely to see an opportunity to use humor or playfulness to extend learning in a Powerful Interaction.

Humor extends learning in many ways. First, humor is play for the brain. It makes the brain work in new ways. Humor often involves playing with language — for example, tongue twisters, silly rhymes, and puns. Through humor, children can develop phonological awareness and add words to their vocabularies. As children learn to use humor to interact with others, they are learning a lifelong social skill.

Let's look at how humor develops across ages and stages of development (McGhee 1979):

Babies laugh when their special people do out-of-the-ordinary things.	**Toddlers** laugh at mix-ups.	**Preschoolers** laugh at nonsense, intentional mistakes, and exaggerations.	**School-age children** laugh at verbal humor.
Goofy dances	Shoes on heads	"You're a silly-billy!"	Knock-knock jokes
Sticking out their tongues	Bananas as telephones	"Can I have a pandwich?"	Word plays
Foolish noises	Little coat on big person	"I want some mud juice!"	Riddles
Silly mouth sounds	Pointing to an eye when the grown-up says "nose"	"You have a square head!"	
Funny faces	Calling people by wrong names	Picture of a giant mouse	
		Loud pretend crying	

Tips for Introducing Humor in Interactions

After a good laugh together, the stress of the day can diminish, a cheery mood can replace a sour one, and a new spurt of energy can appear. Not surprisingly, humor and laughter are often a part of Powerful Interactions.

Seek out playful moments with each child. Follow a child's lead or be the leader. When a child laughs, find out what is tickling her funny bone and join the fun. Once you know what makes each child laugh, you'll be able to have humorous interactions that will surely get a giggle. Here are some suggestions:

When in doubt, sing! Silly songs are sure winners in the laugh category, and they are a great way to play with words and language. Brain researchers have discovered that exposure to music and singing is necessary for the healthy development of language and communication skills (Schiller 2010).

Ms. Sara glances around her classroom of toddlers, most of whom are busy and happy. She notices Koren standing by himself, looking a bit forlorn. She connects by catching his eye. Then remembering his glee as they sang "Boom, Boom, Ain't It Great to Be Crazy" on yesterday's walk, she begins to sing the song as she approaches him. A smile appears on his face, she sits on the floor next to him, they take turns singing lines of the song together for a few minutes and share a good laugh!

REALITY

Every so often, do a Me Check and tune in to the mood that you are expressing to children. Have you smiled today? Or laughed? Have children seen your playful side?

CHECK

Bring toys to life! Fostering children's oral language development and conversation skills are among the most important responsibilities you have as a teacher. Some children may be more comfortable talking to a favorite toy than to you. Try giving a silly voice to a doll, a puppet, a stuffed animal, a truck, a ball, even a puzzle piece. Make them have a conversation with the child!

Watching 3-year-old Salia play silently with her favorite baby doll in the dramatic play area of his classroom, Thomas decides to connect by sitting in a low chair beside her. He picks up a different doll, then extends her learning. Using a high-pitched baby voice, he makes his baby doll talk to her baby doll. As the two babies take turns "talking to each other," Thomas and Salia dissolve into giggles!

Play copycat! Imitation games make children laugh and they are a good way to extend children's skills. You can focus a copycat game on whatever skill a particular child needs to work on — certain sounds or words, a physical skill, counting, or drawing can be made into a copycat game. And don't forget to take turns being the leader!

Ms. Doris scans her classroom of 4-year-olds and notices Marco making a pattern block design with the yellow hexagons and the red trapezoids. Ms. Doris connects by sharing her observation of how much Marco enjoys playing with the pattern blocks.

She decides to extend his learning by initiating a copycat game as a way to introduce other blocks into his design: "Hey, Marco, will you play copycat with me?" Marco smiles and says, "Sure, Ms. Doris!" Ms. Doris says, "You can be the leader first and then I'll take a turn." Each time Marco adds a block, Ms. Doris pretends to think really hard and tells Marco he made it too hard. He laughs out loud. When they swap roles, Ms. Doris introduces different pattern blocks and Marco adds them to his design without hesitation.

REALITY *Perhaps you don't think of yourself as a "funny" person. Don't worry! Begin by taking children's lead. Pay attention to what makes them laugh and start there. We think you'll find that young children are an easy audience for your budding* **CHECK** *sense of humor.*

Laugh it up with language! Young children are learning language at an amazing rate. They are captivated by new words and new ways of putting them together. When you make up new words, rattle off nonsense rhymes, do funny finger plays, recite playful poems, and read children's books that have a sense of humor, you make the world of words an exciting and fun place to play. Listen to Theresa's conversation with 5-year-old Jade at the snack table.

> **Theresa:** "Jade, I see you have a banana for snack today. Let's give it a new name. Let's call it a *fanana*. How do you like your *fanana*?"
>
> **Jade:** (grinning) "I love my *fanana*!"
>
> **Theresa:** (winking) "Okay, you're eating a *fanana*. What's Davey having for *pnack*?"
>
> **Jade:** (laughing) "He's having a *bapple*!"

Make merry with movement! When you encourage children to use their bodies in new and interesting ways, you support their gross motor development. And because brains and bodies are closely linked, you are giving them a mental workout, as well. Fiddling fingers, twinkling toes, shaking shoulders, leaping legs, active arms, and bouncing bodies create joy and learning for dancers of all ages!

> Some energetic music plays on the boom box and 8-month-old Samuel crawls toward Ms. Bea. "Are you coming to ask me for a dance, Mr. Samuel? I'd love to have this dance with you!" She kneels down, lifts him up on his feet, holds onto his hands, and helps him dance by moving his body parts in many different ways. By the time the music ends, both Ms. Bea and Samuel are gasping for breath in between their laughing!

How's It Going?

Humor is a wonderful way to extend children's learning. Look for clues that tell you that your funny and enjoyable Powerful Interactions are having an impact.

Children may be more joyful and happy.

- Babies will pay attention to people who are laughing and having fun.
- Toddlers may begin using silly rhymes and words or bring their favorite funny books to you at story time.
- When you suggest playing a copycat game with pattern blocks or color cubes, preschoolers may get excited because they know they are about to have fun while they learn the names of shapes and colors and positional words.

REALITY

CHECK

When using laughter and humor as part of a Powerful Interaction, it is mandatory that *both* people are enjoying the moment. For example, sarcasm is never appropriate with young children. They interpret your words literally and do not understand that you are kidding around.

As the adult, you must be sensitive to the child's experience. Your sense of humor might be going over the child's head. The child might not be in a playful mood. The child might not feel comfortable enough with you to relax and laugh. Your observation skills are your best detection tool for figuring out when, where, how, and with whom to laugh, be playful, and have fun.

You may be laughing more. Perhaps you're using humor to redirect children's challenging behavior, to break the ice with a very shy child, to release the tension of a stressful day, or to give yourself an energy boost.

You may observe singing, laughing, and dancing happening. Or you may find you're playing a CD of silly songs more often. Some children have favorite silly songs and beg to hear them regularly. You might hear laughing children making their toys "talk" to each other.

Remember: *Add laughing and humor to your pedagogical toolkit to extend learning during Powerful Interactions.*

Ask Questions

Questions have the power to turn children's brains on and get them thinking in new ways. As you read what other teachers say about the art of asking questions, what comments resonate most for you?

Use what you know about children and what they are doing at the moment to ask questions that encourage them to examine and describe, explain their thinking, or make a link.

- *Over time, I've become more in tune and comfortable with the conversations I have with children. I'm learning what kind of questions to ask children so I can learn more about what they know and how they think.*

- *I've really worked hard to ask questions that get children talking about their experiences. I've had some success. Children are more open, and I'm able to hear their ideas.*

- *My coach filmed me and a child playing with LEGOs. I was so surprised to hear how many questions I asked and how fast I asked them. The child didn't even have time to think about them, let alone respond!*

Knowing the kinds of questions to ask and how to ask them is an art that requires time and attention to master.

Questions and Learning

The questions you ask affect what children learn from you and what you learn about them. Compare these two examples:

> After reading a story to a group of 3-year-olds, Ms. Adams asks, "Did everyone like that story?" In unison, 15 voices reply, "Yes!"

> During choice time, Ms. Zucker approaches Yasmine, a 4-year-old in her group and asks, "Yasmine, what did you think of the story we heard at story time today?" Yasmine responds, "I liked it when the puppy licked the little boy."

Ms. Adams asked a yes/no question to a whole group of children. Ms. Zucker asked a thinking question in a one-on-one situation. Ms. Adams's question prompted a unison chorus of a single word, while Ms. Zucker's question prompted Yasmine to reflect on the story and express her opinion.

Asking Questions during Powerful Interactions

In a Powerful Interaction, you pause to be present, then intentionally make a personal connection with the child, simultaneously moving the child's learning forward in a small, yet purposeful way. Therefore, the questions you ask and how you ask them during a Powerful Interaction make a difference in both the child's feelings toward you *and* the child's thinking and learning. Let's take a closer look.

Here's a Powerful Interaction story about Jamilla and 3-year-old Hanson. First, Jamilla tells us what was happening just before the Powerful Interaction began:

> "I saw Hanson next to the water table, watching Mattie play. I looked around the room and everything seemed pretty calm. I realized that Hanson and I didn't really know each other yet, because he started in the program only a few weeks ago. I thought it might be a good time to get to know him a little better and try to get a sense of his language development, so I went over and pulled up a low chair beside his wheelchair."

Then the Powerful Interaction begins. Pay attention to how Jamilla connects with Hanson and then uses questions to extend his learning.

Jamilla: "Hi, Hanson. You've found something pretty interesting to watch here at the water table." (Jamilla waits a moment.) "Mattie's scooping up water and pouring it through a funnel into that big pitcher." (Jamilla is quiet for another moment, and Hanson leans a little closer to her. She points to the pitcher.) "Look at how full the pitcher is getting! I wonder what Mattie will do when the water gets to the very top?" They watch together in silence.

Jamilla: "Do you and your little sister like to play in the water?"

Hanson says "Shara," and nods yes. Suddenly, his eyes are open wide and he points to Mattie.

Jamilla: "Oh, look, you noticed what Mattie is doing now that the pitcher is full! What is she getting ready to do?"

Hanson: (laughing) "Dump it!"

Jamilla: "I think your prediction is right! Do you think all the water will fit in that bowl?"

Hanson: (shrugs his shoulders) "I don't think so!"

The Art of Asking Questions

Like the three teachers quoted at the beginning of this chapter, Jamilla is practicing the art of questioning during Powerful Interactions. Notice the strategies she uses:

- **Alternate between silence, commentary, and questions.** Jamilla is very careful not to bombard Hanson with questions one right after the other. She pauses frequently. She uses an "I wonder" statement to prepare Hanson for a question: "I wonder what Mattie will do when the water gets to the very top?" Using "I wonder" gets Hanson thinking but is less threatening than actually asking him a question that he has to answer.

- **Tailor the questions to the child.** Jamilla is also aware that she and Hanson don't know each other very well yet, so she wants the interaction to feel safe and comfortable for him. She asks questions that he can respond to easily. She begins with a simple yes/no question: "Do you and your little sister like to play in the water?" She asks him a gentle prediction question: "What is she getting ready to do?"

- **Offer a manageable challenge.** Even though Jamilla's questions are gentle and not very challenging for Hanson, they still engage his brain and cause him to observe more closely and make predictions. "Do you think all the water will fit in that bowl?"

Like all Powerful Interaction strategies, the art of questioning requires paying attention to what you already know about the child, observing the child in that moment, and individualizing what you say and do accordingly. Jamilla did just that, and you can, too.

Choosing Questions Intentionally

Knowing about different kinds of questions and having a repertoire of questions ready make it easier for you to choose the most appropriate question for the child and the situation.

Some questions require a quick and simple answer, using one or two words:

● "How many fingers do you have?"
● "What color is your ball?"
● "Do you like the soup?"

Other questions require responses that take more time, thinking, and words:

● "How do your fingers help you?"
● "What do you notice about your ball?"
● "What does the soup taste like?"

Sometimes you want to invite a child to examine and describe:

● "What do you notice about that shell?"
● "What did you see on your way to school today?"
● "What does ___ look (feel, sound, taste, smell) like?"
● "What's the same about these two balls?"
● "How is your tower different from Kyle's tower?"

At other times, the situation may call for a question that nudges a child to explain his thinking:

● "How did you decide to group these buttons together?"
● "How did you feel when George gave you a hug?"
● "Which part of the story was your favorite? Why?"
● "How did you figure that out?"
● "Why do you think that happened?"

Maybe the situation is ripe for a question that invites a child to make a link between the unfamiliar and the familiar:

● "Has something like this ever happened to you? What was it?"
● "What does this remind you of?"
● "Have you done anything like this before?"
● "Where else have you seen this?"
● "Who does that remind you of? Why?"

Tips for Asking Questions

Observe first. Take time to be with the child. Use mirror talk to show interest in what she's doing. Get on her wavelength before asking questions.

Give a signal. Let the child know you are about to ask a question. Point to your head or pretend to put on your thinking cap.

Be patient. Give the child time to think. Either be quiet for a moment or let the child know with words that you are okay with silence: "I'll wait while you think." ... "Take a quiet thinking moment."

Remind yourself. Hang "question starter" signs around the room: What Do You Notice? ... How Did You Figure That Out? ... How Are They the Same/Different? ... What Does _____ Remind You Of?

Individualize. Some questions can be responded to in one word; others in a few or many. Some require more complex thinking than others. Take the child's cognitive and language development into account when choosing questions. Relate questions to what the child is interested in at the moment.

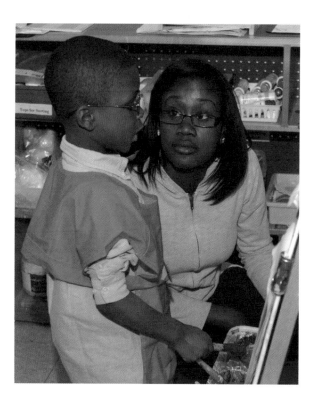

Scaffold. If the child has a hard time responding to your question, offer some help — a choice of responses, a hint or clue, a word or two, or a simpler question.

Acknowledge varied responses. Depending on the question and the situation, a child might shrug, smile, nod, take an action, tell you a story, answer a different question, use one word, or use lots of words.

Extend and enjoy! Questions often launch wonderful conversations. Take time to talk and think together:

> "Tell me a little more about your idea. I never thought about it that way; where did you get that idea?"

> "The other day, you told me something else about that. You're really thinking about it these days. What else have you thought up?"

How's It Going?

Watch and listen to children for clues that you are mastering the art of choosing and asking questions in your Powerful Interactions. You might notice that children begin to

- Anticipate your questions

    "Do you want me to tell you what I notice?" … "Should I explain my thinking?" … "I'll tell you how I figured it out."

- Ask some of the same questions you ask

- Ask their own questions

- Respond to your questions in more complete and complex ways

You may also notice that you are beginning to enjoy the Powerful Interactions that result from your improving questioning skills.

Remember: *Asking questions during your Powerful Interactions with children is an art that takes time and practice to develop. Ask questions that gently stretch the child to think and respond in new ways.*

Link the New
to the Familiar

Have you ever listened to someone speak and thought afterward, "Well, that went in one ear and out the other." Or read something and thought after a few pages, "I have no clue what I just read!" When we don't have a way to make personal meaning out of what we see, read or hear, we tend not to take it in. Or if we do take it in, we don't hold on to it very long.

Relate new concepts and skills to children's interests, experiences, or something they already know.

Do you have a story to tell about a learning experience you had in which you had a difficult time relating it to something you already knew or to something of interest to you? Exchange stories with a colleague.

Making Links and Learning

Like adults, children learn better when content is meaningful to them. Content is meaningful when it relates to something familiar — an interest, an experience, or something children already know.

Meet Lucia! Eager to learn, Lucia enters your classroom with a large tote bag over her shoulder. You might predict that Lucia has a snack or maybe a stuffed animal in her tote. But instead, imagine that her bag is full of attitudes, preferences, interests, knowledge, abilities, memories, experiences, and understandings that she has collected in her young life. In her bag are all the things that feel familiar to her. She's bringing HER life into YOUR classroom!

As Lucia's teacher, you have a tote bag, too! In your bag is everything you want and need Lucia and the children in your program to learn while they're with you. This strategy for extending learning is about how you can help children like Lucia see links between the familiar things in their bags and the new things in your bag.

Linking Knowledge during Powerful Interactions

Children need your guidance to bridge the gap between their life experiences and all the new things they are trying to learn in school. This "bridging" makes it easier for them to take in, understand, remember, and use the new ideas, knowledge, and skills. Creating learning connections as you interact with children leads to Powerful Interactions.

As you read this story about Ms. Natasha, think about how she uses this Powerful Interaction to help 30-month-old Victor make connections so that it's easier for him to learn new concepts.

Victor is painting a very colorful picture. Deciding this is a good moment to help Victor learn more about colors, Ms. Natasha pulls up a chair and joins him at the easel.

Ms. Natasha: "Victor, you've used so many colors in your painting!"

Victor beams a broad smile in her direction.

Ms. Natasha: "You must be thinking of lots of different things as you paint." (She points to brown paint on his picture.) "I see some brown. I wonder if you were thinking about your brown dog?"

Victor: "Doggy."

Ms. Natasha: "Yes, your dog, Chaser! You love your brown dog, don't you? I also see some orange here?" (She points to the orange on his painting.) "You must have been thinking of something orange. Do you have something orange at home?"

Victor: "Pun'kin." Victor points to a pumpkin on one of the classroom tables.

Ms. Natasha: "I should have guessed that you had noticed our new pumpkin. You notice everything new! I'm curious about one more color in your painting. What about this big spot of red? Your mommy was wearing a red sweater this morning."

Victor: "Mommy."

Ms. Natasha: "Your mommy has a beautiful red sweater! She's so lucky. I wish I had a red sweater, too! I can't wait to see what other colors you'll put in your painting, Victor. I'll be back to look in a few minutes."

Reflect on what made this a Powerful Interaction. Think about how Ms. Natasha made a personal connection with Victor. What did she do and say throughout the interaction to continue building her relationship with him? How did she link the new to the familiar in Victor's life to guide his learning a small step forward?

How did you do? Compare your analysis with the one below.

● **Personal connection**

Ms. Natasha uses mirror talk to connect with Victor. She tells him what she sees him doing: "Victor, you've used so many colors in your painting!" Victor feels reassured that Ms. Natasha likes him. He can tell that she's interested in what he's doing and appreciates his efforts. She opens the door to strengthening her relationship with Victor and moving his learning a small step forward.

- **Relationship building**

Throughout this Powerful Interaction, Ms. Natasha continues to make her relationship with Victor deeper and stronger. "You love your brown dog, don't you?" She lets Victor know that she is tuned in to what is important to him. She reminds him that she knows he really loves his dog, Chaser.

"I should have guessed that you had seen our new pumpkin. You notice everything new!" Ms. Natasha recognizes Victor's strengths by letting him know that he's very observant. "I can't wait to see what other colors you'll put in your painting, Victor. I'll be back to look in a few minutes." Ms. Natasha assures Victor that she'll stay in touch with him.

- **Links to extend learning**

Throughout this Powerful Interaction, Ms. Natasha creates learning connections for Victor, linking his own life experiences and new color concepts. She connects the color brown in Victor's painting to his beloved brown dog. She guides Victor to connect the color orange with an object he had observed in the classroom. She connects the color red to the color of his mother's sweater.

Tips for Building Links

Here are some suggestions to help you link the new to the familiar for children during Powerful Interactions:

Build links between read-aloud stories and children's own life experiences.

"When you go for a ride in the car with your family, you wear a seatbelt, right? The little girl in this story doesn't want to wear her seatbelt. Let's see how she solves that problem."

"Last week you were upset about moving to a new house. This story is about a little boy just like you. He doesn't want to move either."

Build links between new classroom materials and familiar materials.

"Here are some new blocks for the block area. How are they the same as the other blocks? How are they different?"

"I remember when you told me that you like to play Candy Land with your sister. I think you'll like this new game because you have to match colors just like you do when you play Candy Land."

Build links between new and familiar words.

"The little bear in this story just said he was exhausted. Have you heard that word before? When you go home after a long day at school, you might feel REALLY tired. You could say, 'I'm exhausted!' Try saying, 'I'm exhausted!'"

"There's a new obstacle course on the playground today. Remember the last time we had a new obstacle course? At first, you were hesitant. You watched kids and then you tried it. You might be hesitant today, too. It's okay to watch first if you feel hesitant."

Build links by asking "connection questions" that help children relate familiar experiences and new knowledge and understanding.

"What does this remind you of? Where else have you seen/heard this?"

"Has something like this ever happened to you before? What happened?"

"Who does that person remind you of? Why?"

How's It Going?

As you build links between familiar and new learning during Powerful Interactions, you may notice that children begin making their own learning connections without as much guidance from you. Look for clues that individual children are doing this; for example

A 2-year-old, noticing a picture of a child wearing the same color shirt he is wearing, smiles and points to both shirts.

A 3-year-old says "my daddy" when you read about Papa Bear.

A 4-year-old notices a new clock in the classroom and says, "That's almost like the clock at my house, except that one's black and mine is blue."

Remember Lucia's Tote Bag: *Each child comes to you with a different collection of life experiences in his or her tote bag. Your job is to find out about the contents of their bags so that you can help children build links between what they have already experienced and the new knowledge and ideas that you want to teach them.*

A DAY
IN THE LIFE OF
MS. PAT

You met Ms. Pat at the beginning of this book, in the chapter A First Look. Now, as you near the end of the book, she invites us to listen in on her reflections on her day of Powerful Interactions.

Ms. Pat has 15 children in her preschool class. Although she has everyday interactions with children all day long, she strives to have at least three Powerful Interactions each day. This way, by the end of the week, she can be sure to have had at least one meaningful and intentional interaction with each of the children.

As you'll see, she finds that taking 10 minutes at the end of each day, after children have left, is a good time to think about the day's Powerful Interactions, to plan how she'll follow up on them, and to identify three children for tomorrow's Powerful Interactions and begin anticipating them.

After seeing the last of her preschoolers depart, Ms. Pat grabs a cup of coffee, pulls up a chair at the art table, and settles in for her daily 10-minute mental replay of the day...

Let's see … All the kids were here today. During arrival time I was able to connect and have a Powerful Interaction with Dashawn. It made me feel good because he tends to be quiet, and I have to be careful not to overlook him.

Today our eyes met and we smiled at each other as his dad told about how they played soccer over the weekend. When his dad left, Dashawn showed me how he kicked the ball. It was funny when he said, "It went 100 miles." "That's a long way," I told Dashawn.

We've been doing lots of measuring lately. To extend his learning, I decided to start a game about distance. I took a giant step and asked, "How far do you think I stepped?" We marked and measured my step using a block. My step was six blocks long. Then Dashawn took a step. When the next child arrived, I explained I was going over to greet her at the door. When I looked back, Dashawn was measuring the snack table with the block. He'd asked Marcellus to join him.

Then later this morning I had my second Powerful Interaction, with Jo-Jo outside. He's not a big talker either, but he sure knew about how the lever on a dump truck works. I've got to stop by Mrs. Hall's room to borrow her copy of *The Little Dump Truck* (by Margery Cuyler) for reading time tomorrow. Hmmm. That's a nice way to build on his interest. And, I'll ask to borrow two more hard hats for the dramatic play area.

After snack this afternoon, I found another moment for a third Powerful Interaction. Maya was at the easel and wanted orange paint, like her smock. "I have a problem," she told me. I listened. It was a great opportunity to help

her build a link to a discussion we had a while back about color mixing. I asked her if she remembered what colors she might mix to make orange. Rather than get frustrated, like she often does, she started experimenting. What delight registered on her face when, after her second try, she mixed the yellow and red! I snapped a photo and will add the caption now. I'll be sure to share it with her mom in the morning.

Tomorrow's plan will be to have Powerful Interactions with Arjun, Leah, and Trina.

Here are Ms. Pat's notes …

3-22

Everyone here today. PI's with Dashawn, Jo-Jo, and Maya

Dashawn: Arrival time. Connected with him while his dad was here. Learned he likes soccer. Extended learning about measurement. He spent 10+ minutes measuring classroom objects on his own. Later told me about how big they are. FOLLOW UP: Be sure to take soccer ball outside. Find new objects to measure outside.

Jo-Jo: Knows a lot about dump trucks. FOLLOW UP: Get dump truck book from Mrs. Hall for reading time. Talk about levers and other parts of the truck.

Maya: Got interested in experimenting with the colors. FOLLOW UP: Show painting and tell story to her mom. Take advantage of other problems to extend Maya's learning through experimenting.

3-23

Arjun: Try harder to quiet my mind to connect. Put out the birds puzzle he likes.

Leah: Ask Leah's dad when they last Skyped with her mom (deployed). Watch for time to play with sounds and words and make up songs about going away and coming home — something Leah likes doing with mom.

Trina: Invite her to tour new obstacle course, so she knows she can get through it wearing her leg braces.

POWERFUL INTERACTIONS: YOU MAKE THE DIFFERENCE!

At the beginning of this book, we made you a promise. We said that incorporating Powerful Interactions into your practice would bring about two important outcomes — children would be learning more and you would become a more effective teacher. Throughout the book, you've read about research highlighting the positive impact of your interactions with individual children. As you reach this final chapter, we hope that you are experiencing these outcomes for yourself.

What are some changes you're observing in children's engagement and learning? Step back and appreciate the ways you're becoming a more effective teacher.

Without **YOU**, there are no Powerful Interactions! So in this final chapter, we want you to think about ways you can take care of yourself to ensure that you can be present, connect with children, and extend their learning in Powerful Interactions every day … day after day.

Powerful Interactions take ENERGY and CONFIDENCE.

Energy — Keep Your Cup Filled!

Working with young children is wonderful, but it also can be exhausting. Resolving to have a Powerful Interaction with a few children every day shouldn't feel daunting. Now, at the end of this book, it should seem not only doable but satisfying and rewarding, as you see children more engaged, motivated, and learning.

But Powerful Interactions do take energy — physical, mental, emotional, and creative energy — to decide how to connect with children and extend their learning in personal, meaningful, and purposeful ways.

How can you be sure you'll have the energy for them?

Imagine This!

Imagine your personal energy as filling an 8-ounce cup. Whatever your day's activities, whether you try waking up earlier or staying up later, you only have 8 ounces. That's all you get.

Your daily energy

Now imagine you're starting your day. After a good night's sleep, let's say your cup of energy is two-thirds filled. A healthy breakfast and your favorite song on the radio add another quarter cup. Maybe your cup gets topped off by a big hug from your spouse, or a smile from your daughter as she gets on the bus. So off you go to work. … Then you step in a puddle on the driveway in your new shoes, or get caught in traffic, or remember that you left your lunch bag on the kitchen counter.

slowly gets depleted

You're still on your way to work, but some of your energy may already be draining away.

Throughout the day, some people and some situations can deplete your energy. Others can energize you and refill your cup.

and you need a refill!

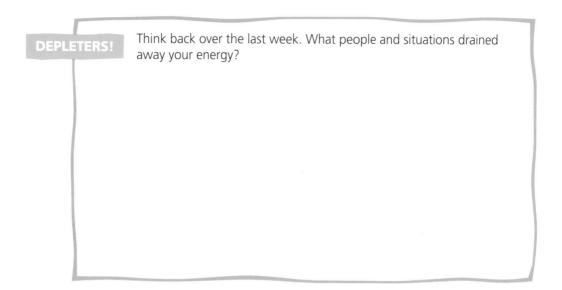

DEPLETERS! Think back over the last week. What people and situations drained away your energy?

ENERGIZERS! Think about what gives you energy during the day. Jot down three energizers that help refill your cup.

You can't always avoid or control the depleters, but you *can* pay attention to when your energy is running low. As one teacher said, "I know my cup is down to 1 ounce when tying a child's shoe for the third time feels like a major project."

When your cup of energy is running empty, it's hard, if not impossible, to organize yourself to have a Powerful Interaction with a child. It's difficult to take that moment to pay attention, listen, and make good decisions about how to respond rather than react. Moreover, you need energy to take full advantage of your internal riches — your passions, your sense of humor, your curiosity and creativity, your knowledge and skills, and your willingness and flexibility to change and grow.

You need energy to take the three steps of a Powerful Interaction. Your energy fuels you to **be present** so you can decide how to **connect** and **extend learning** in the most effective ways.

But, once you've had a Powerful Interaction, you can say to yourself, "Yes, I *do* make a difference!" Feeling effective as a teacher is itself an energizer — it fills your cup.

To be able to transform a couple of everyday interactions into Powerful Interactions for a few children every day, you have to keep your cup of energy as full as possible all the time.

Get into the habit of paying attention to how much energy is in your cup. If you feel like it's getting low, seek out energizers — people and situations — and pour yourself a few ounces.

Here are just a few ideas for energizers to have up your sleeve or in your back pocket for when you need them. Think about which ones will work best for you, and add others of your own:

KIDS SAY AND DO THE FUNNIEST THINGS!

- While eating fresh pineapple for snack, Rachita (age 22 months) asks, "Can you take out the picks and the pokes?"

- Nathan (age 30 months) stands looking at two statues in the park. "They are not talking. They are stuck."

- Justine (age 4) arrives wearing new purple gloves. I say, "Oh, Justine, what lovely purple gloves." She responds, "No, I'm not wearing gloves. These are mittens. When they grow up they'll be gloves."

- Aaron (age 6½) wants to be a paleontologist when he grows up. He knows all about mastodons, and he wishes he could have one in his backyard. He asks his mom, who is a doctor, "Do paleontologists have to be on call at night?"

Look for humor!

- Jot down the funny, amusing things children say and do. Read them when you need a boost.
- Share funny stories from your work with children with a colleague, with a child's family, or with your own friends and family at home.
- Seek out that colleague who always makes you laugh.

Set priorities.

- Make a to-do list. Divide the items into "high," "middle," and "low" priority. Write them down. … Then cross off all the low-priority ones.
- Put a star next to the three most important high-priority items you want to accomplish this week. Make sure they are specific, discrete tasks (e.g., "Write three sentences on the Center's blog about collecting rocks yesterday" instead of "Communicate more with parents").
- Pick just one of the three to start with … and do it. Take deep satisfaction from crossing it off the list with a fat black marker!

Add personal touches to your space. This makes it easier to relax and be yourself.

- Make sure you can sit comfortably with children at their level, so you can listen, observe, and talk with them.
- Add a few things to your teaching space that make you happy and give you a lift — a favorite poster, a photo, a poem or quote, a vase of flowers, a fresh mango to enjoy during your break, or a CD you love to dance to (we imagine you'll find no shortage of dancing partners).

Create an energy exchange. Sometimes it's hard to refill your cup of energy all by yourself. Find ways for the members of your team to energize one another, which contributes to the energy of the whole group.

- Take turns bringing in flowers for each classroom, or for the break room.
- Alternate bringing in healthy, tasty snacks to share one day each week.
- Check in with each other regularly. (For example, are you stiff after a weekend of hiking or gardening? Talk together about including stretching exercises into movement time.)
- Share responsibilities for dealing with stress.
  - Take turns shadowing that child who needs extra-close supervision, the toddler who bites or the 5-year-old who hits.
  - Tune in to each other's cues or set up some signals so you can step in to lend a hand if another teacher needs it or share an amazing thing a child in your room is doing.

Make energizers part of your daily routine.

- Make sure you and the children do joyful activities each day — sing, read stories, go outdoors, make muffins!

- Share the hobbies you like to do — dancing, listening to music, cooking, reading, watching birds, telling stories, playing the guitar, woodworking, jogging. Find ways to work these activities into your lesson plans, either for the whole group or a small group. Adapt as necessary, make them safe for children, and enjoy!

- Put up your feet and close your eyes for 10 minutes during your lunch hour.

Confidence — Watch Yourself in Slow Motion!

It takes confidence to turn everyday interactions into Powerful Interactions. To be present, you have to be willing to step back, take an honest look at yourself, and adjust to the children rather than expecting them to always adjust to you. When you are confident, you trust yourself to make decisions about how to connect with each child, even those who push your buttons. And finally, with confidence, you will try a new strategy to extend a child's learning, observe to see how the child responds, and make modifications when necessary.

Confidence comes from reflecting on what you do and acknowledging the importance and effectiveness of your work.

Imagine This!

Imagine watching sports on television. Thanks to instant replay, we get to see pivotal moments in a game replayed again and again, as commentators analyze each little action in the quarterback's touchdown throw, the outfielder's spectacular catch, or the tennis player's amazing serve.

What would it be like if the important work *you* do as a teacher was given this same kind of attention?

After all, what you say and do with young children influences how they feel about themselves, their attitudes toward learning, how they develop, and what they learn. What "game" could be more important than helping to shape the person a child grows up to be?

What if, like that quarterback, outfielder, or tennis player, you could watch and analyze instant replays of your interactions with children as a tool for further improving your already-expert performance?

If you could review your own "training films," you might

- Realize that 8-month-old Freddy looks worried when he hears you talking with another child in a stern voice, and decide to pay more attention to how you sound when talking with children

- See how 30-month-old Chris settled down as you put your arm around him and engaged him with a toy

- Discover that when you are concentrating, the expression on your face looks annoyed, which may be why Eddie, age 3, sometimes backs away

- Notice that you distracted Sophia, age 6, when you commented, "I see you are writing about your kitten," and decide that next time you will wait to comment until she looks up at you or pauses in her work

Right there in your classroom you can create opportunities that are like slow-motion replays — chances to play back what you do and say as you interact with the children. You can reflect on the decisions you make, appreciate your skills, see how new strategies are working for you, and consider ways to refine your practice. Here are some ideas:

Keep a journal. Replay your Powerful Interactions in writing by reflecting on and recording your insights, observations, and plans.

Talk with colleagues. Exchange stories of your Powerful Interactions with colleagues. Discuss what worked, how children responded, and what you might adjust the next time.

Use videotape. Ask a colleague to record you having Powerful Interactions. Watch the videos alone or together. Pay attention to small details. For example:

- The pace and tone of your voice, body language, and facial expressions

- How the children respond to you

- Ways you personalize your interactions

- The variety of vocabulary and language you use

- The content focus of your interactions (e.g., are your interactions always about the same things — counting, colors, or the alphabet?)

"When teachers tell the stories of their professional experience, they often change how they see themselves as teachers."

— Meier & Stremmel 2010, 4

Work with a partner. Ask a trusted person to observe you. Afterwards, have her tell you what she saw, describing your actions and words as you interacted with the child. Often is it hard to see yourself accurately. Your actions may be quite different from your intentions. This peer collaboration can give you valuable feedback and help you raise questions and change your practice.

Join with colleagues in a professional learning community. Using this book as a guide, you might decide to do some focused action research about Powerful Interactions with colleagues. At regular intervals, you can read sections of the book together, practice strategies in your classroom, and come together to share your reflections.

Share your stories at our website. There you will find an evolving conversation about Powerful Interactions, as well as resource materials:

www.powerfulinteractions.com

As you become more aware of your be present moments, how you connect with children, and the ways you choose to extend their learning, you'll improve your effectiveness, and your confidence as a teacher will grow. Once you're thinking about Powerful Interactions yourself, it's only natural you might begin thinking and talking with your teaching partner and other colleagues. You've begun a conversation!

Keeping the conversation going will help you get better at achieving Powerful Interactions. It also will help other teachers begin journeys toward Powerful Interactions of their own. In fact, we think keeping the Powerful Interactions conversation going and growing will help the field of early childhood education!

Supporting a Broader Conversation — What action steps could you and/or others take to grow the Powerful Interactions conversation?

One Last Word

Well, you're finally at the end. We hope you've enjoyed this book, and will return to it often as you try out its Powerful Interactions strategies and tips. We've offered you lots of interesting ideas — perhaps some are familiar and some are new.

What has stayed with you?

- A strategy that you feel confident about?
- A teacher from one of the examples?
- A child you met in a story?
- A photograph or two?
- An idea that might help you with a particular challenge you're facing?
- Something that made you smile or laugh?

Whichever strategies become a natural part of your practice, we hope you remember this: Your Powerful Interactions DO make a difference! *

REFERENCES

Beck, I.L., M.G. McKeown & L. Kucan. 2002. *Bringing words to life: Robust vocabulary instruction.* New York: The Guilford Press.

Birch, S.H., & G.W. Ladd. 1997. The teacher-child relationship and children's early school adjustment. *Journal of School Psychology* 35 (1): 61–79.

Bodrova, E., & D.J. Leong. 2007. *Tools of the mind: The Vygotskian approach to early childhood education.* 2d ed. Columbus, OH: Merrill/Prentice Hall.

Bowlby, J. 1982, orig. 1969. *Attachment and loss: Vol. 1, Attachment.* 2d ed. New York: Basic Books.

Center for Social and Emotional Education. n.d. *School climate research summary.* Online: www.schoolclimate.org/climate/documents/schoolClimate-researchSummary.pdf.

Early, D., O. Barbarin, D. Bryant, M. Burchinal, F. Chang, R. Clifford, G. Crawford, W. Weaver, C. Howes, S. Ritchie, M. Kraft-Sayre, R. Pianta & W.S. Barnett. 2005. Pre-kindergarten in eleven states: NCEDL's multi-state study of pre-kindergarten and Study of State-Wide Early Education Programs (SWEEP). NCEDL Working Paper. Chapel Hill: The University of North Carolina, FPG Child Development Institute, NCEDL. Online: www.fpg.unc.edu/~ncedl/pdfs/SWEEP_MS_summary_final.pdf.

Epstein, A.S. 2007. *The intentional teacher: Choosing the best strategies for young children's learning.* Washington, DC: NAEYC.

Furrer, C., & E. Skinner. 2003. Sense of relatedness as a factor in children's academic engagement and performance. *Journal of Educational Psychology* 95 (1): 148–62.

Galinsky, E. 2010. *Mind in the making: The seven essential life skills every child needs.* New York: Harper.

Gallagher, K.C., & K. Mayer. 2008. Research in Review. Enhancing development and learning through teacher-child relationships. *Young Children* 63 (6): 80–87.

Hamre, B.K., & R.C. Pianta. 2005. Can instructional and emotional support in the first-grade classroom make a difference for children at risk of school failure? *Child Development* 76 (5): 949–67.

Hart, B., & T.R. Risley. 1995. *Meaningful differences in the everyday experience of young American children.* Baltimore, MD: Paul H. Brookes.

Hirsch, E.D. 2003. Reading comprehension requires knowledge—of words and the world. *American Educator* 27 (1): 10–13, 16–22, 28–29.

Howes, C., & S. Ritchie. 2002. *A matter of trust: Connecting teachers and learners in the early childhood classroom.* New York: Teachers College Press.

Hyson, M. 2008. *Enthusiastic and engaged learners: Approaches to learning in the early childhood classroom.* New York: Teachers College Press; Washington, DC: NAEYC.

Jablon, J.R., A.L. Dombro & M.L. Dichtelmiller. 1999/2007. *The power of observation for birth through 8.* Washington, DC: Teaching Strategies; Washington, DC: NAEYC.

McGhee, P.E. 1979. *Humor: Its origin and development.* San Francisco: Freeman.

Morrison, F.J. (discussant). March 2007. Contemporary perspectives on children's engagement in learning. Symposium presented at the biennial meeting of the Society for Research in Child Development. Boston, MA.

Munro, S. 2008. Opportunity lies in teacher-child interaction. *The Education Digest* 73 (6): 46–48.

Myers, S.S., & A.S. Morris. 2009. Examining associations between effortful control and teacher-child relationships in relation to Head Start children's socioemotional adjustment. *Early Education and Development* 20 (5): 756–74.

National Research Council. 2001. *Eager to learn: Educating our preschoolers*. Committee on Early Childhood Pedagogy. B.T. Bowman, M.S. Donovan & M.S. Burns, eds. Commission on Behavioral and Social Sciences and Education. Washington, DC: National Academy Press.

National Scientific Council on the Developing Child. 2004. *Young children develop in an environment of relationships: Working paper no. 1*. Center on the Developing Child, Harvard University. Retrieved from www.developingchild.net.

National Scientific Council on the Developing Child. 2007. *The science of early childhood development: Closing the gap between what we know and what we do*. Center on the Developing Child, Harvard University. Retrieved from www.developingchild.net.

O'Connor, E., & K. McCartney. 2007. Examining teacher-child relationships and achievement as part of an ecological model of development. *American Educational Research Journal* 44 (2): 340–69.

Pawl, J.H., & M. St. John. 1998. *How you are is as important as what you do . . . in making a positive difference for infants, toddlers, and their families*. Washington, DC: Zero to Three.

Phillips, D., K. McCartney & S. Scarr. 1987. Child-care quality and children's social development. *Developmental Psychology* 23 (4): 537–43.

Pianta, R.C. 2000. *Enhancing relationships between children and teachers*. Washington, DC: American Psychological Association.

Pianta, R.C. May 25, 2010. Connecting early education to K–3 through professional development for effective teaching and learning. Testimony to the U.S. Senate Health, Education, Labor, and Pensions Committee hearing: ESEA reauthorization: Early childhood education. Online: http://help.senate.gov/imo/media/doc/Pianta.pdf.

Ridley, S.M., R.A. McWilliam & C.S. Oates. 2000. Observed engagement as an indicator of child care program quality. *Early Education and Development* 11 (2): 133–46.

Schiller, P. 2010. Early brain development research review and update. *Exchange* (November/ December): 26–30.

Seplocha, H., & J. Strasser. 2009. Using fanciful, magical language in preschool. *Teaching Young Children* 2 (4): 17–19.

Sigel, I.E. 1993. The centrality of a distancing model for the development of representational competence. In *The development and meaning of psychological distance*, eds. R.R. Cocking & K.A. Renninger, 141–58. Hillsdale, NJ: Erlbaum.

Stetson, C., J. Jablon & A.L. Dombro. 2008. *Observation: The key to responsive teaching*. Washington, DC: Teaching Strategies.

Vick Whittaker, J.E., & B. Jones Harden. 2010. Teacher-child relationships and children's externalizing behaviors in Head Start. *NHSA Dialog: A Research-to-Practice Journal for the Early Childhood Field* 13 (3): 141–67.

Vygotsky, L.S. (author), & M. Cole, V. John-Steiner, S. Scribner & E. Souberman (eds.). 1978. *Mind in society: The development of higher psychological processes*. 14th ed. Cambridge, MA: Harvard University Press.

SOLANO COMMUNITY COLLEGE

COORDINATOR: SABRINA DRAKE
707-864-7000 X 4639